FORGOTTEN WELSH HOUSES

With all good wishes from Michael Tree

By Michael Tree and Mark Baker

Front and Back Covers: Troy House, near Monmouth

Title Page: The early seventeenth century section of Edwinsford, Talley, Carmarthenshire
Contents Page: Iscoed, Ferryside, Carmarthenshire

Published in 2008 by Hendre House Publishing
© Michael Tree and Mark Baker

Graphic Design by Tom Pollock, Excellent Design, Anglesey
Tel: 01248 490792 • www.excellentcreative.co.uk

Printed by Cambrian Printers, Aberystwyth

ISBN 13 - 9780955968402

Forgotten Welsh Houses

Contents

Dedicated to
Rosemary who provided the key
to dream dreams which created reality anew

It is now twelve years since I launched my own Heritage Preservation Trust, latterly known as The Prince's Regeneration Trust, and at that time pledged that I was not prepared to sit back and see this country's legacy of great historic buildings needlessly squandered – especially when, with imagination, they could become real assets to their local communities, offering job opportunities and a focus for local regeneration schemes. The intervening years have seen some notable successes but, far too often I fear, many opportunities have been lost. I am glad, therefore, that the authors of this book have drawn together such a compelling list of current houses at risk.

I am sure that readers of this book will share my concern to realize that such a large number of our heritage assets in Wales are in such danger. This clearly represents, at best, a waste of tangible assets and, at worst, the loss of an all-too-significant part of our common heritage. Ensuring that abandoned buildings, whether they be houses, churches, farm buildings, civic buildings or industrial buildings are brought back into use is the best way to guarantee their survival. In terms of building types, it is industrial buildings and agricultural buildings that have some of the highest percentages of structures recorded as at risk. However, it is probably the wide range of historic houses described in this book that present us with our greatest regrets and conservation challenges.

It is truly astonishing that included in the buildings at risk listed in this book are several truly great buildings such as Ruperra Castle, Troy House and Piercefield, by Sir John Soane. Many of these buildings are also situated within the most romantic and beautiful landscapes Wales has to offer. Two very beautiful houses come to mind in particular; Iscoed, overlooking Carmarthen Bay and Neuadd Fawr, set against a magnificent mountainside near Llandovery. These buildings exemplify architecture of outstanding quality enhancing magnificent natural landscapes, and it will be an utter tragedy, if not a complete scandal, if these, amongst others, cannot be saved. Such a sublime combination of architecture and landscape is very rare indeed and, surely, appropriate uses can be found to save these buildings?

Given the extent of past losses recorded elsewhere, I sincerely hope that all concerned will not hold back any effort in encouraging new owners to share the blessings and the burdens of the stewardship of our historic buildings. Furthermore, I hope that some of the underlying and tangential issues which have been so clearly indicated here will be carefully considered by those in authority; those who could make a considerable difference to the future survival rate of our heritage, based upon the knowledge we have gained and the lessons we have learned from the cause of past losses and the loss of past causes.

Introduction

Hafod, Aberystwyth
A tragic loss – Hafod, near to Aberystwyth was one of the earliest examples of Gothick revival architecture in Wales and a prominent exponent of the picturesque movement. Up to World War Two this was one of the great Welsh estates, but shortly thereafter was stripped of its fixtures and fittings before eventual demolition.

When Michael Tree moved back to Wales several years ago to rescue a pretty 'pocket estate' in the Conwy Valley, he assumed that the extent of the risk of losing notable heritage property was now probably quite small. The huge losses Wales had already suffered were well recorded in Tom Lloyd's 1986 book, the Lost Houses of Wales, which illustrated over three hundred houses, gardens and parks which had disappeared in a short space of time during the twentieth century. In spite of this, there were only fifteen or so listed at the end of the book as still being at risk, although presumably savable. So 'all seemed quiet on the western front…'

Gradually, though, it emerged that perhaps things were not quite as they seemed. The great house of nearby Kinmel Park had lain fallow for many years (and, at the time of writing, it still is), magnificent Gwrych Castle had been needlessly abandoned to squatters and vandals, and then Hafodunos, that Victorian jewel in the crown of Welsh heritage, was burnt to the ground by arsonists in 2004. Naturally, one could not help thinking that perhaps the reality of the matter was rather different to the perception. By chance, it became apparent that Cadw (now part of the Welsh National Assembly with special responsibility for the built heritage) had similar thoughts, and indeed had responded by offering every County Council a large grant to get all listed buildings thought to be at risk in their areas properly surveyed, in order to establish the nature and extent of the problem.

Little by little, these lists were obtained by the authors, often by serving formal 'Freedom of Information' notices on the County Councils.

When they arrived, however, the authors could barely believe what they saw; for example in Gwynedd alone (excluding Snowdonia National Park), there were over three hundred and fifty heritage properties at risk. These included four listed Grade I, twenty listed Grade II*, and three hundred and thirty one Grade II - an astonishing number. The lists included most types and structures from country houses and stable blocks, an orangery, forts, locomotive houses and fine garden features, and so on. In effect, they incorporated all that could be said to contribute both to the visual patina of our countryside, and its historic association which, in turn, make up part of our national identity.

In effect, therefore, what we are looking at are some unparalleled opportunities for Building Preservation Trusts and individuals to whom their home is far more than a 'machine in which to live' and who seek those spiritual delights so readily provided by architectural excellence, historic association, appeal and high amenity; all of which are synonymous with our historic buildings, parks, gardens and landscapes. This should, of course, be considered against a background of what is arguably an unprecedented increase in property values over the last sixty years or so, which has affected Wales rather less than, say, the Home Counties. Finance alone is only a small part of the story, however, so there should be bargains enough for all interested parties. The other side of the coin includes ready access to a countryside that is still largely unspoiled from Victorian times, which can be an easy route into a vibrant national and local culture which is so distinct from other parts of the UK.

Whilst many of the properties shown here have irresistible appeal, few of them appear to be on the market for sale and thus require tenacious follow-up by those who are genuinely interested in both acquiring a new home and rescuing part of our national heritage at the same time. Nevertheless, a word of warning; this scenario will not continue forever. Little by little, challenges may well be taken up and thus be unavailable to future generations. Now, therefore, is the time to act if one is to secure a home which otherwise might be unrealistic.

It is appropriate to remember the advice given in America one hundred and fifty years ago: 'go west, young man, to find the land of opportunity.'

Success Stories

Those of you who actually take up the challenge and delight of rescuing one of these great properties will have the comfort of knowing that you are not the first to embark on such an adventure. There have, in fact, been a number of brave souls before you who have taken their future into their own hands and, with a little luck, turned a problem building into a notable family home or business. Here we are thinking of Cornelia Bayley at Plas Teg, near Mold, who turned a nigh-on ruined Jacobean mansion into a home and a tourist attraction of great distinction. Not only did the regional economy benefit from the considerable costs of renovation in terms of the employment of local labour and the purchase of building materials, but here we are twenty years later and the house is still earning its keep by opening regularly to the public. In fact, many a B&B in the immediate area thrives from the need to accommodate those who have travelled large distances to visit this great house.

Another North Wales success that springs to mind is Bodysgallen near Llandudno, which, under the care and devotion of that conservation guru Richard Broyd, has been sumptuously fitted out as one of the great hotels of the UK, attracting guests to North Wales from all over the country as well as from abroad. Here again the economic benefit to Wales is considerable: this is a big business and thus big benefit for the local community.

In Mid-Wales, one cannot think of successful rescue operations without mentioning Auriol, Lady Linlithgow. Her rescue and renovation

Plas Teg, Mold

A remarkable early seventeenth century house, built by the Trevor family, to a most advanced design for the time, with an arresting silhouette. Last used as the family's primary seat during the 1930s, it was never fully used or cared for again until 1986 when Mrs Cornelia Bayley restored Plas Teg back to a sumptuousness that rivals most others. What an influence this has been for Trevor Hall, Cairness House and Gwydir Castle.

of the delectable Bryngwyn a few years ago has become an exemplar that many of us try to follow, but few achieve. Again, this is a property that is now earning its living by contributing fulsomely to both the national and local economy, through a wide variety of events.

Equally, when one travels to South Wales, rescue operations and the name of Steve Weekes of Penhow Castle are synonymous. He took on this building many years ago when it was no more than a derelict ruin, which he then proceeded to turn around to the point where it became a very significant national tourist attraction. Equally, it is a delight to mention two other very distinguished schemes by foresighted local authorities, each in its own way being quite outstanding. First is the rescue of the mighty Morgan family house of Tredegar, Newport, by the local council. This has done them huge

credit, particularly in terms of organising their priorities by making room for their own heritage. Likewise, the rescue of the equally mighty Margam Estate core, near to Swansea, by the local authority is a huge credit to them too. The Orangery there is one of the greatest in Europe, whilst the house itself which was burnt out in the 1970s is being re-roofed and is gradually coming back into beneficial use once again.

One can mention many more (e.g. Pickhill at Wrexham, Bettisfield at Hanmer, Peniarth near Tywyn); these illustrate convincingly that 'where there is a will there is a way.' Even if a rescue project takes many decades it can, in the meantime, still provide huge challenges and pleasures for its lucky owners. Conversely, simply throwing cash at a project is not only wasteful but can be destructive and is rarely the answer. There is never any substitute for the owner's passion, commitment and enthusiasm, which have so often, in the right combination, become great cash substitutes for rescuing heritage properties in danger of being lost.

It is perhaps stating the obvious when one hopes that this book may prompt some of its readers to enter the noble fray, take up the opportunities and challenges of rescuing Welsh houses 'at risk,' only a few of which have been mentioned in this book. In total they represent something like 17% of listed buildings in Wales. For those who are as determined as they are passionate, we would strongly advise that they obtain copies of the buildings at risk registers from the County Councils in those areas of their interest and to plod through them, item by item, in search of serendipity. This is clearly the opportunity of a lifetime where no stone should be left unturned and no refusal accepted at face value. But please remember that this book is not a passport to trespass: most properties are privately owned and must be respected as such.

Methodology

There has been no attempt to record each and every potential opportunity for rescuing heritage items included in the county council lists; space alone would preclude this. Therefore, the items included represent a personal list that has appealed to us for one reason or another; to some it may indeed be a curious selection but that is for others to judge. However, we feel that in a broad sense, it fairly reflects the wealth of opportunities for rescuing heritage opportunities there are in Wales as a whole. We hope also that it will be useful to official bodies, insofar as it attempts to give some idea as to the general extent of the problem of heritage at risk in the 21st Century.

Bodysgallen, Llandudno
An ancient seat of the Mostyn family that seems to have grown out of its own foundations, occupying an elevated site in an ancient park, with a very sophisticated formal garden, and welcoming modern obelisk which is seen for miles around. This whole property came perilously close to degradation, prior to a rescue operation of the finest calibre by that saint of the heritage world: Richard Broyd. The house is now a first rate hotel and an asset for north Wales tourism.

We have tried to restrict ourselves almost exclusively to buildings on the various 'at risk' registers even though there have been strong temptations to include others as well and in a few notable places we gave in to sentiment. On the other hand, there have been many instances where, for whatever reason, we have judged it best to omit certain cases of particular sensitivity. Nevertheless, our selection has not been easy as we recognise that it is every person's right to maintain their buildings, within reason, as they see fit; thus, just because a building is shabby it does not necessarily mean it is at risk of being lost, although it could nevertheless be at the start of the downward path to actual dereliction and loss. Thus, if nothing is done by way of emergency maintenance and security is withdrawn, then in our experience the time scale for the building to be lost is about twenty years. This is particularly the case with the larger houses that are perhaps more at risk of destruction through vandalism. This does at least give some framework within which decisions should be taken.

We are glad to say that we have visited every single building mentioned and, wherever possible, we have only taken photographs with the owner's permission. In a number of instances, though, especially where buildings have been abandoned and there has been no immediate owner from whom to seek consent, we took photographs from public highways or other convenient vantage points. In some instances, for whatever reason, current photographs are simply not available; therefore, we sought whatever was available from local residents, the National Library of Wales and the Royal Commission of Ancient and Historic Monuments for Wales.

It cannot be emphasised too strongly to interested parties that the first contact point for any of the properties shown in this book should be the County Conservation Officer of the county concerned. It should be noted that, inevitably and thankfully, some properties visited will have been rescued by the time this book goes to print. Or at least they may have been taken over

Bryngwyn, near Welshpool
This deceptively sized house is a joy which could have featured in 'Pride and Predjudice', and yet it could easily have been lost having been empty for over forty years. But no, along came the very determined Auriol, Lady Linlithgow, who undertook here one of the most successful rescue operations of the time. It is now a family home again of great distinction which is available for a wide variety of functions, and which is thus an important aspect of the local area.

Bettisfield, near Wrexham

This ancient seat of the distinguished Hanmer family was huge, and more like a small village then a house, so quite understandably it was reduced in size after World War Two, but to a not very pleasant mish- mash of Regency and Victorian elements, which nevertheless failed to save it becoming hopelessly derelict by the 1990s. Then along came the redoubtable Mrs. Cornelia Bayley of Plas Teg fame, who demolished the Victorian parts to reveal a fine country house by the Wyatts, complete with exquisite plasterwork, fixtures and fittings. What a triumph of aspiration over despair!

by new owners, even though the building still remains at risk. The situation is not static but entirely fluid. Again, this book is not intended as a passport for trespass. Both space and time precluded us addressing every property at equal length. The difference between the main list and the Gazetteer is merely personal choice: all properties mentioned are as important as each other in their own way.

History

Having had just a glance at the extent of the challenges and opportunities in this book and remembering Tom Lloyd's record of houses lost since 1900 in Wales, one is bound to ask 'why has one whole section of the national heritage suffered so dramatically'? Insofar as the houses are concerned, there are parallels elsewhere in Europe. Nevertheless, the whole-scale abandonment of such wonderful items of the national heritage is bound to raise both the question 'why?' and of 'how come?'

Not surprisingly, in these circumstances, the causes for this great change can be seen to result from many interrelated causes, most notably perhaps two World Wars that accelerated social and political evolution and brought about the need for high taxation, at times of an unprecedented extent. For the first time since the civil war, such huge changes were experienced repeatedly in the twentieth century, as opposed to once every hundred years or more previously. Additionally, we had normal social evolution with the passing of the various great reform acts, which ushered in various levels of democracy and the consequential diminution of locally based power sources. No longer was it the duty of local educated people to govern a county through the magistracy; the work simply became too much and too complicated, hence the establishment of county councils introduced in 1889. Add to this a policy of free trade, which encouraged the importation of huge quantities of cheap corn from the prairies of America and the technology that created refrigerated ships bringing large quantities of meat from South America and the Antipodes. Add again to this the continuing need for taxation to cover all the outgoings of a modern democratic state and you can see the inevitability of 'the country interest' coming under increasing pressure to share the burden of modern financial planning.

Under these circumstances, the decline of the landed proprietors both large and small was perhaps inevitable and indeed recognised by some well before the turn of the twentieth century. What was, therefore, an inevitability in times of peace, was accelerated by the two World Wars of the last century in which so many sons of heritage properties served and died. Understandably, in many instances the grieving parents at home, facing the loss of succession, huge political change, death duties and other large increases in taxation, simply gave up the ghost. In so many cases, the continuity of a certain way of life with adequate staff and other helpers ended slowly but surely, and with it, the sustainability of the homes in which they lived and worked. Some certainly did manage to change and survive, although for many the

P. Sandby R.A. pinx!   W. Watts sculp.

EDWINSFORD, the Seat of R. Banks Hodgkinson Esqr.

Edwinsford, Talley

Here is a challenge for those who would be gods: this historic house of the Williams's, subsequently Hamlyn Williams Drummond of Hawthornden, sits so well on the banks of the Cothi as to entice the attention of J.M.W.Turner. Sadly now very derelict, but still worthy of rescue. This was a great example of fine welsh architectural achievement of the early eighteenth century.

Gwrych Castle, Abergele

Abergele's Gwrych Castle was fully functional and open to public as a tourist attraction right up to the mid-1980s. Following sale to an absentee owner, unbelievably the building was stripped of its interior and what was left heavily vandalised. After many years of campaigning for restoration by Mark Baker, work is now well underway and hopefully the phoenix will once again arise from the ashes.

financial and intellectual demands of a modern state were beyond them but their gorgeous homes still survive.

Not surprisingly therefore, such properties were often unwanted and had little or no value, especially in a market then flooded by such property. Many is the time that a visit to such properties finds that the owners had departed but their furniture, books and carpets, even their clothes were still in place. In so many instances this was, in effect, a melancholy end to a continuity of occupation that frequently went back over one thousand years in any one spot. The loss to our local history has been considerable as a result.

Today, Wales is still peppered with homes built by those who were patrons of the arts, had received a fine education and possessed cultivated tastes. This, not surprisingly, resulted in huge care taken with the selection of sites and with the style and detail of the buildings subsequently erected. All of this has come down to us as our common heritage. Yes, we have lost a lot, but it is now high time for current generations to see again the opportunities our forbears have bequeathed to us, and to rescue them again both for our own community benefit and as an endowment to those who are to succeed us.

Opportunities

Most of the properties we have illustrated here represent great opportunities to rescue heritage items at far less total cost than those located, say, in the Home Counties. Potentially they can provide a family with the chance to endow itself for many generations to come by buying and rescuing something special in areas of almost overwhelming Arcadian beauty. Of course it has to be recognized that not so long ago such properties had little value for many reasons, not least of which on account of their location. Now, thanks to the computer, motorways, and aircraft, even the deepest Cardiganshire for example can be reasonably accessible. As can be seen here in this book, these properties range from chapels to barns, mansion houses and delectable farmhouses. These may be bought as a permanent home or to trade and sell on, or simply as a financial investment to be rented out, but the quality, variety and quantity of such buildings is arguably unique in the UK. Finally, remember that tenacity and patience usually achieve great rewards, and can be fine substitutes for lavish funding.

Pitfalls & Failings

In some ways, there are few things worse than getting emotionally carried away with a scheme mostly for all the right reasons, and then for it to go wrong at a later stage for reasons that should have been anticipated at the start. This aspect has only been touched upon here, as it could easily warrant many chapters in its own right. Nevertheless, our basic words of caution include the following:

1. One of the first things to do is to always find out the history of the property from local people; visiting the local pub, speaking to adjoining neighbours and local Building Preservation Trusts usually pays dividends. Most often you will find local people who have known the property for upwards of fifty years and thus know all of its problems. Bad neighbours can drive you out and make your chosen property unsaleable; only rarely can one change them.

2. Engage a local valuer to report to you with all the perceived problems, e.g. the field in front of the house not owned and not available for purchase. This can look innocent enough when you buy, but it is entirely a different matter when, eighteen months down the line, your friendly local farmer decides to use it for farrowing pigs.

3. Check the local plan at the planning office for any possible long-term threats such as road widening, farm buildings on a mammoth scale, nearby industrial development, and anything else that could affect your amenity. Any and all possible planning threats imaginable should be discussed with the local planning officer.

4. Consider very carefully what extra land it may be advisable to acquire. This can always be a realistic possibility if the vendor and an adjoining owner are friends and both wish to see a sale to a good and a kindly new owner, but once that sale has gone through, you can do little more than forget it.

5. Take much care initially with the way you approach your neighbours in order to avoid getting off on the wrong foot. It is far better to be a little distant to begin with and get to know your neighbours gradually than to blunder in and quickly generate their antipathy towards you. Secure your own boundaries as soon as you take possession, remembering that 'good boundaries make good neighbours.'

6. Consider planning the work of rescue over such numbers of years as makes sense for you. Equally, consider short-term mothballing of certain areas and the question of emergency repairs aimed at keeping all options open for a long time to come. Ensure that there is adequate finance available to establish yourself at the property of your choice, even if this is insufficient for undertaking the entire list of works envisaged. The basic minimum should

allow you to inhabit some of the property in normal conditions of comfort and keep the rest 'ticking over' until you can get around to it.

7. Engage an engineer who is familiar with heritage studies, and specifically check for impending catastrophic collapses.

8. It has to be accepted that there is a possibility of the house of your dreams being owned by a company that in reality wants the building to be demolished to open the way for a more lucrative use. Thus, any dialogue is impossible. In which case discuss the matter at once with the local authority which may consider compulsory purchase if you will enter with a 'back to back' agreement with them.

Rescue Options

There are any number of possible rescue options for a building at risk, limited only by human ingenuity. For any building project, security is a major issue that needs to be attended to before anything else. Maybe a part of the property can be quickly converted into a caretaker's flat, a cottage on site may be available, or one might have resort to a caravan or similar temporary structure. This is going to be of prime importance, especially when valuable building materials and tools are brought on site.

Gwydir Castle, Llanrwst
Seat of the famous Wynns of Gwydir, this was the centre of a huge estate until well into the twentieth century, when disaster struck: the historic contents of the house were sold off just before a savage fire left much of the house as a roofless shell, for most of the thirties and early forties. Then against all the odds roofs were put back by the local bank manager, Arthur Clegg in his retirement. But squatters eventually moved in, and Gwydir became a squalid dive, before being taken over by Peter Welford and Judy Corbett. They have transformed it, even bringing back original panelling from the Bronx, that had been sold to William Randolph Hirst.

The very first objective should be to make the property both wind and watertight. This includes temporary drainage both above and below ground and possibly constructing a temporary roof over the whole property. Whilst this can be expensive, it can also enable work to continue on the exterior of the building virtually uninterrupted by inclement winter weather. This too is the time to identify all structural defects and dry rot to stop them getting any worse.

Whenever possible, comfortable accommodation, even on a very small scale, should be created within the building and temptation to use, say, a nearby cottage should usually be resisted. All too often such a cottage can become permanent with contingent detriment to the main house.

Try to avoid being over ambitious by attempting to restore more of the property than is financially prudent in the first instance. Once the building is wind and watertight, one then has the option of deciding how much to restore and when. For example, once a significant part is habitable then areas like say, a surplus third floor can be left indefinitely.

After this has been decided, it will then be possible to assess how the work is to proceed; whether to employ a large overall contractor or to issue a series of small sub contracts, or to employ direct labour. In any event, it is usually necessary to undertake a certain amount of 'opening up' to ensure that guaranteed fixed price contracts can be entered into whenever possible. This may not always be possible but should be treated as an objective.

When costs are established, care needs to be taken as to whether the building works need to be done in phases and, if so, over how long a period. Generally, it is wise at least to reserve the provision to nominate specialist tradesmen. On any detailed restoration project, it is also advisable for the employer to engage his own 'clerk of works', who should be on site for the entire duration of the building work and whose loyalty is to the employer alone.

An owner needs to consider whether he/she will get up to speed with technical items or employ someone else to do so on their behalf. The former is by far the better choice. We have assumed that a property is already connected to the main services; if not, then such connection should be one of the very first things to do, remembering that a bore hole can be a quick solution to problems of water supply. It is worth recording, however, that in many instances of successful rescue operations, the new owners have mitigated their costs by becoming specialists in the field of conservation and employed their own team of builders direct. In almost every instance, regardless of the availability of funding, owners often tend to be 'hands on' people.

Rescue Team

Any owner needs to consider with the utmost care the extent of the professional team that is needed on a job and how much use they intend to make of each member. Much depends upon the technical expertise a particular owner has personally to hand; however, to a greater or lesser extent, the team will consist of the following:

• **Conservation Architect** – This is perhaps the most critical of all the appointments, as one has to recognise the specialist knowledge that will be essential for a successful outcome of a conservation rescue project. Care needs to be taken to establish whether the conservation architect is in control of the whole project, part, or employed on a time basis. In any event, all fees need to be agreed in advance and to be capped. Equally, ensure that no other member of the team is given a blank cheque concerning fees.

• **Structural Engineer** – This again is a vital appointment and should go to somebody who is fully conversant with heritage buildings and who can come up with innovative, cost effective solutions to structural problems.

• **Quantity Surveyor** – Again, it is vital that the quantity surveyor should be fully competent in heritage rescue projects. A good budget will be essential and especially useful to monitor payments so as to verify progress and potential cost over time.

• **Project Manager** – This is sometimes required on a large job, who should be engaged on little more than a monthly basis with the ability to terminate their employment at short notice as and when appropriate.

• **Builders** – Select builders who are conversant with the practices of conservation (and the use of traditional materials) and provision should be taken to be able to nominate specialist workers such as grainers, French Polishers, painters, and ornamental plasterers, joiners, plumbers, electricians, etc.

• **Interior decorators** – Try to ensure that there is a certainty as to costs, both overall and in terms of what is to be purchased. It is suggested that an hourly rate is established, that there is an obligation to buy in goods at best available price, and that receipts should always be supplied. Generally, interior decorators should be able to demonstrate an in-depth knowledge of historical precedent to achieve a coherent overall effect.

• The last, but most important of all, is the building owner, who should be in a position to act as an informed client at all times.

Trevor Hall, Llangollen
Trevor Hall, rescued by Michael Tree, between 1987 and 1999, after many years use as a farm building following a fire that had burnt the roof off. Supposedly the birthplace of Tudor Trevor in 940 AD, this photogenic house now earns its keep as the most delightful venue for weddings, and holidays, with exquisite views over the Vale of Llangollen.

Garthewin, near Abergel

Home of the Wynnes of Garthewin, this house illustrates how, with the right owner, a tradition of several hundred years can be continued. Sold by the family during the mid-1990s, it was eventually purchased by Michael Grime, who has sensitively restored the mansion and estate buildings, as well as undertaking a major conservation exercise of the park and gardens. The whole property now looks as well if not better than it has for centuries.

Getting Going

Whilst one may have a clear idea in the mind's eye what one wants to do, and thus feel as though one is able to start on site right away, unfortunately, if one is not to be filled with regrets in the future, there is quite a lot of preparatory work to be done apart from those items already mentioned. These include the following.

• **House History** – Commissioning a history of the house and its owners at a very early stage can pay dividends in terms of establishing the way the house was used and the way it has evolved. It could also enable one to locate past items of consequence that could perhaps be returned, e.g. a portrait of the builder of the house. It may be that a photographic album of the property can be located and so forth.

• **Archaeological Survey** – An archaeological survey of the house can also pay dividends in terms of identifying colour schemes, papers and fabrics that could perhaps be used again under certain circumstances (an archaeologist at the initial clearing of the site can be very important). The essential issue here is to obtain as much information about the history of the house as possible, so that nothing is needlessly or unwittingly harmed or destroyed in the future rescue scheme. Equally important is for the gardens to be surveyed in detail in order to fully understand its evolution and to guide future proposals.

• **Planning and Listed Building Consent** – Inevitably, these take time. It is therefore worthwhile going to see the planning officer and others at the earliest possible date to both avoid delay and to be aware of local sensitivities. Ideally, the preparatory work should be sufficiently detailed so as to ensure that eventually the application goes through almost 'on the nod.'

• **Local Officials** – Very frequently, properties to be rescued are very prominent in their own area. It is therefore wise and courteous, at the earliest possible stage, to seek out as many local officials as possible to acquaint them with your aims and ambitions and to find out theirs. Once they are convinced that the new owner is competent, straightforward and has laudable aims and objectives, delays and disruptions with official consents can be greatly minimised.

• **Grant Aid** – This is always an attraction in theory, but do remember that such funds are now scarcer than ever, and that it usually only ever goes to the very best examples that can be labelled as 'outstanding'. There are usually conditions attached, such as the need to use specialist specifications, certain building materials, and to employ certain specialists. Various charitable bodies can offer grant aid to private rescue operations, but, generally speaking, do not do so if the property concerned is a private house.

• **Local Labour** – One of the most important things when taking on such a rescue operation is to be able to identify the skills available in the local area. Contacts within the local community are therefore important and can often result in much specialist labour being available in the immediate vacinity, conveniently and at reasonable cost.

• **Contents** – Most families will have left behind or sold some contents, which may or may not fit into the rescued house on grounds of size, style and taste. Consideration therefore should be given to supplementing an existing collection by further purchases. Generally speaking, the most economical way of doing this is attendance at local and national sale rooms, where the quantity and quality of items on offer are little short of astonishing, although it must be said that this can be time consuming, and additional renovation costs have to be taken into account. Otherwise, buying straight from the antiques trade is an option, although sometimes rather an expensive one. In any event, it pays dividends to study paintings and drawings that were contemporary with your house in terms of age and style, particularly as a quarry for new ideas. Again, one is driven by the need for a certain degree of coherence within the property which will appeal to some but not all. Here again the overriding need is for an owner to undertake the role of an informed client, and who may well strike up a good relationship with a recognised dealer specialising in art from specific geographic areas. Do not forget the local art dealers and consultants who can be a mine of information about historic contents and can look out for relevant items for new owners. Some new owners will wish to explore the route of entirely contemporary furnishing or a combination of the two: the principles are the same. Cultivated patronage is what it is all about.

Progressing from Day One

Assuming that you have found the property of your choice, managed to infect your family with your own level of enthusiasm for it as well as negotiated satisfactory purchase terms, then the following points might be of assistance.

It may well be that family solicitors are perfectly capable of undertaking the transaction on your behalf. However, it is well to check that they really are experienced in this field of property, that they will undertake the work for a fixed price, and that they are aware that under no circumstances should they lose the sale on your behalf. It is absolutely vital that time limits be set and agreed with the purchaser at the very beginning, so that the matter is not allowed to drift. Given that this may be one of the most important transactions of your life, it is important that you monitor progress at least twice weekly and that the vendor's estate agent is kept informed in order to avoid any suspicion that your interest is on the wane at any time.

that the building you intend to rescue is probably unmortgagable you have the compensating freedom of being able to buy without the mortgage company breathing down your neck and refusing security because, say, there is a degree of instability that can easily be put right but which nevertheless is a complication that they will not wish to contemplate. This means, too, that you will need to depend upon your own judgement, sometimes perhaps against your solicitor's advice. When looking at the wider picture you will need to decide whether it is in your best interests to buy the property or walk away. This is where good judgement and firm resolve are indispensable, but even at this stage 'rose tinted' spectacles can play a part.

Once your offer has been accepted and your solicitors have been instructed, it is wise to visit the property regularly to ensure that you get to know it in its finest detail before it is conveyed to you. These visits can become highly entertaining family outings, and plenty of photos can ensure that no change takes place at the property between offer and contract. It is also a regular confirmation to the vendor that you are determined to conclude the matter on the terms agreed.

There are few things that lift the spirit more from the first moment than well-kept grounds. In the early stages, the gardens do not have to be fully up and running, but enough should be done to ensure that the owner and family could enjoy the amenities of the property from the beginning. This too, is the time to get to know your neighbours and their families, where doubtlessly a junior member may be available to assist with some of the gardening work.

As the job progresses, an owner should endeavour to be aware of what is happening on a daily basis, through phone calls or personal visits. The owner should ensure that any problems with budgeting and progress are revealed through budgets at weekly meetings, which need only take fifteen or twenty minutes at the most; these meetings should give warning of any problems before they become serious and allow evasive action whilst it is still possible.

All owners should be aware of the three fundamental principles governing the conservation of historic buildings: 'Detailing, Detailing, Detailing!' The most cursory visit to any National Trust house reveals the importance of this statement. Generally, it is not the size of the purse that makes the difference between a sad, forlorn rescue and one that has seen to be a success at every level. What usually makes the difference is the owner's enthusiasm, commitment and ingenuity, without which a successful outcome is impossible.

Soft furnishings can be a significant element in the wider scheme of things if allowed to be so. Again, it is worthwhile to remember the old saying that generally it is better to use inexpensive material voluptuously, rather than expensive material sparingly. Indeed, if sourced with ingenuity, excellent fabric is usually available from wholesalers at modest cost.

The successful restoration of original colour schemes are an achievement in their own right, if they survive in anything like an original state. Here again it is critical that a detailed survey is done so as to find out what has been the case in the past; whether there are precedents that are advisable to follow, or a previous scheme of considerable distinction which has been covered up and could be reinstated. It is also important to consider the historic qualities in the property and whether they can be married to the owner's personal taste. In any event, it is a very wise choice to take care that none of the previous schemes should be destroyed by stripping the surface of both wood and plasterwork. If previous schemes are not obliterated in this way, then future generations retain the option of making fundamental and continuing reviews of decoration upon the basis of reassessed evidence.

In some ways, these properties were of greatest cultural value when occupied by their founding families with the original contents in place which so often reflected the nature of the communities from which they came and for whom they served. Thus, all too often, such properties were museums of local history of fine quality. Some new owners may consider it important to maintain the option of continuity by acquiring for the property items that had been there historically, which thus marked a milestone in its history and that of the surrounding area; for example, a portrait of the last of the line of a particular family branch. Such artefacts returning to the area can be of great significance in terms of local history and continuity. In this regard, a study of previous Wills can be a goldmine of sources for current whereabouts of particular items. For example, there is an ink well moulded from the hoof of the last ox to plough at Edwinsford; in that house it was priceless but elsewhere it is no more than a curiosity of little worth.

The issue of obtaining any form of grant aid should be addressed at the earliest stage, and many government and EEC grant schemes have restricted windows of opportunity. Very often local authorities can grant aid for rescue of endangered buildings, and of course, DEFRA and the Assembly may well be able to assist with the agricultural side of the rescue operation. From the outset, it is worthwhile considering the use of a specialist Charitable Trust that can open many funding doors especially if there is to be wide community participation.

Tangential Issues

• **Grant Aid by the Welsh Assembly Government (Cadw grants)** – This is the traditional source of funding, whether from Cadw or from what used to be the WDA. They are hugely valuable and generally come with great advice, as well as modest conditions.   Millions each year are distributed this way, but one cannot help but think about how much less might be given, had decisive action been taken at the start of the problem. For example, Gwrych Castle may now be in receipt of very large funds indeed, and thank goodness this is the case. On the other hand, only a fraction of this would have been needed twenty years ago had resolute action then been taken to stop the catastrophic dereliction. So, if we 'fast forward' the issue to countless of the properties included in this book, now is the time to help out the likes of Golden Grove, Pool Hall and Kinmel Hall, not in twenty years time when they could be derelict shells, and the overall cost to the taxpayer could be many times more than it is now.

• **Painting the Picture** – It is perhaps only appreciated by a few, how immeasurably lucky we are to have a wonderful collection of painted images of many of those who commissioned the heritage items we have included in this book. But, sadly, accessibility is problematic; we have no Welsh Portrait Gallery, yet the potential for serendipity is fully illustrated in these pages.

• **The 'Basket Case'** – We have been astonished by the tenacity of some owners in rescuing properties long after the roof has ceased to exist. Thus, there is always hope of a rescue even if the place is a ruined shell– never give up hope even after some of the main walls have come down. An example of this is Bertholey, near Llantrisant, which had been derelict and roofless since 1905. Thanks to the foresight of the current owner, as it is a great home again; thus proving the point that heritage is a dynamic, ongoing, living subject. Also mention must be made here of two exemplars whose significant collapses of fabric had occurred before any work: Alta Bella and Sker House.

• **Rising to the Full Challenge** – Taking on any of the properties featured will be a challenge for whomsoever attempts to do so. But here we would like to suggest the existence of a hidden, implicit and deeply enduring challenge; that the owner really does become the master of the subject to the point where he/she can promote true patronage of the arts in terms of design, craftsmanship and execution which is equal to the lost examples that our forebears achieved. Here, therefore, is the real challenge: to create today items of such excellence that they stand every chance of becoming tomorrow's heritage. It can be done, but remember, you will always be compared against the best that previous generations actually achieved. By so doing you may be able to achieve a degree of immortality!

Sker House, Kenfig
This is one of the most ancient of Welsh houses to come to the very brink of being lost, and indeed a significant portion of it had actually collapsed. Yet against all the odds it was rescued by the Spitalfields Trust through an exemplary conservation exercise.

Post - Rescue Issues

These properties invariably had close connections with the communities from which they sprung and, indeed, were usually very prominent in those communities. As an element of continuity, this seems to be popular with new owners and perhaps can be the means of providing the whole family with spiritual and emotional anchors to a particular area and a particular community, and can enrich both alike. This may be achieved through opening the gardens once or twice a year under the National Gardens Scheme; running a B&B and weddings, encouraging the properties' use on occasions for fundraising events for local charities, or indeed running it as a business for weddings, conferences, etc. Conversely, we have never come across an occasion where there was any advantage to a new owner by isolating the property from the local community; each needs the other.

When the property has been conveyed to you, is perhaps the time to draw up in secrecy a wish list of further acquisitions in the locality that would benefit the property, so that the issue of a ransom price is not encouraged. Inevitably, the extent to which the most rescuable properties have been pared down by sales during the times they had little or no value is regrettable. Thus, there will always be opportunities to create 'added value.' For example, the minimum ideal land holding for most properties of significance amounts to everything within the park walls including the gate lodges, park, home farm (if there is one) and ornamental copses. This can be labelled as the 'golden area' when the ownership includes all of this; but if not, then to an extent one's amenity is in the hands of others and there is the risk of it being the subject of the opinion of the local planning committee or the planning inspectorate as to what is important and what is not. Owning one's own amenity land really is the only sure safeguard against possible future problems.

Some idea should be obtained as to the extent of the building works and particularly what is likely to be spent with the local builder's merchant. This will then enable a new owner to argue successfully for significant discounts for building materials and other supplies. Indeed, for large purchases, in volume terms it is usually wise to run a small tender amongst builder merchants for particular items: Habitually going to one source of supply without checking competitors' prices on a regular basis is usually a recipe for paying excessively in the end.

Securing good relationships with the local authority and grant-giving bodies at the earliest possible date is a real investment in terms of time and trouble. In most instances it is best to understand the way they work, how they deal with problems, whether they are flexible or not, etc, before submitting applications for planning consent or grant aid or whatever.

It is wise to check with all local historic bodies and societies as to whether they are aware of any articles that have been written in the past upon the property. These can sometimes be invaluable in the influence they can exert on renovation schemes.

Now is probably the time to organise the re-routing of any intrusive public services. Electricity poles are usually one of the worst, and have often been located where they are simply because nobody thought the matter through. Nevertheless, this is an expensive exercise and should be undertaken once only, so caution must be taken to ensure that the future is well catered-for in current proposals.

Cefn Mably, near Cardiff
What a miracle that this house has survived: the estate was sold up and the family moved out years and years ago. Thereafter it accommodated a hospital before being gutted by fire, which could so easily have been the end of the matter, but no, the house was subsequently converted into flats, with considerable numbers of luxury houses built in the grounds adjoining. Thus Cefn Mably as a piece of architecture has been saved, but perhaps not as a country house with its setting now gone.

Opportunities for the Future

Understanding the central relevance and influence that our heritage has to the lives of all civilised people is hard to over-emphasise. Effectively, we are the beneficiaries of huge efforts of cultivation from past generations who, to an extent, believed that they had found some universal truths they wished to pass on for the benefit for future generations. The Welsh countryside, therefore, which is so uplifting, is a case in point; it was created by our forebears in pursuit of financial security, sustenance and spiritual well-being. This has produced a countryside of stunning visual beauty not often seen elsewhere, but this was not sufficient in itself. Those worthy people, our forebears, expended infinitely more energy and effort than they needed for themselves so that we, as their heirs, could benefit from their endeavour. This applies as much to the buildings in the landscape as it does to landscapes, parks and gardens. Let us not forget that these remarkable craftspeople who created such beauty and distinction were invariably compatriots who are still with us, laid to rest in our local cemeteries. Rarely, perhaps, do we know precisely who they were in terms of their personal identity, but in terms of the beauty which was the creation of their own hands, they are all around us for the benefit not only of ourselves, but of those yet unborn: they are the most vulnerable of us all. It is their endowment, to which they have every right to look to us as good stewards, that is recorded within these pages.

Let us not forget that these properties actually represent phenomenal opportunities both for owners and for the nation alike. Repeatedly, one comes across skilfully researched reports that highlight quite conclusively the economic benefits such properties play in their community. This is crucial to the financial well-being of the nation. This is also why it is simply not good enough to turn our backs on the real opportunities that these challenges spawn. They represent unused assets that could and should be activated for the benefit of the community at large.

Community Benefits

General community benefits have been mentioned above in passing, but they are nevertheless very significant and are worth recalling in that, once it has been decided to rescue these properties, the benefits that spring to the local community are considerable, including the employment of a local workforce, fostering traditional skills, the financial benefit of the use of local builders merchants and professional advisors, the national and local attraction to which these buildings, when completed, contribute, the value in being a base for fundraising for local charities, their potential for educational links with local schools, the contribution they make to sustaining local shops, traders and bed and breakfast providers and their significance as local and national elements of our common heritage. In effect, they begin to pay their way from day one, and, far from being a burden, are cash generators for the nation and as well as local community.

The Future

Given greater prosperity now than at any time since the first World War, these properties' high amenity value and local distinction are likely to be more and more in demand, both as housing for people drawn to work in Wales and for local people with a passion for history. Thus these 'buildings at risk' should be seen to be not only a national resource but a lifetime's opportunity to acquire now at modest cost, in comparison to the likely value they will have after they have been rescued. Thus, they make good economic sense from the start, provided they are rescued in a professional manner.

Many such properties, through judicious development or conversion, can become thriving small businesses with all the fiscal advantages that this implies for their owners.

Although the rescued building can provide endless pleasure for whole families, it has to be accepted that there will come a day when inheritance by the next generation is inevitable. Current owners will then have the challenge of enabling a change of ownership to take place without it harming that which over the years they have striven so hard to save. In particular, this usually means ensuring that the property is not fragmented into multiple ownership, which could be ultimately self-defeating. So often, an outright sale without injuring the property is better than dividing the ownership between siblings who could be at war with each other and use the property as a weapon. Very often this need not cause a problem, provided that the property is not divided from the outset and compensation in some form or another is ensured for those who do not inherit. Many owners may agree that primogeniture, even in the twenty-first century, has its own advantages.

However, most owners, new and old, will probably agree that, in light of past losses and other depredations, their attitude now is 'never again' should other generations have to face the rescue operations that are detailed herein. In this context, charitable trusts may no doubt have their place, on carefully thought-out terms; in effect many do-it-yourself National Trusts.

To conclude by quoting from Johann Wolfgang von Goethe:

'That which thy fathers have bequeathed to thee, earn it anew if thou wouldst possess it.'

So the best of luck to all our readers, and especially to those few individuals who will take up the challenges of rescuing some of Wales' finest items of national heritage now at risk of being lost. It will be a life-changing and life-enhancing experience to endow future generations with heritage property that have come so close to complete destruction.

Michael Tree

FORGOTTEN WELSH HOUSES

BARON HILL

House Listing Grade – II
Gardens & Park Listing Grade – NOT LISTED
Authority – Anglesey County Council

DESCRIPTION

Baron Hill is one of Wales' most admirable and strikingly situated houses. Sitting above the charming coastal town of Beaumaris, it looks out over renowned medieval fortifications towards the Irish Sea, Menai Straits and Snowdonia. This notable site has been occupied by a dwelling since the early part of the sixteenth century, when an advanced Renaissance house was built in a similar vein to Plas Teg, Mold and Foxhall Newydd, Henllan. Like Foxhall, it was apparently never fully completed, but was finished to such a degree that it served as the principal residence of the Bulkeley family up to the 1770s, when it was substantially rebuilt. Samuel Wyatt was employed by the 7th Viscount Bulkeley to carry out the works and what resulted was in honour of his former master,

Robert Adam. Wyatt's Baron Hill survived well into the 1830s when Henry Harrison, an architect, refurbished the house. Tragically, when work was nearly completed, fire ravaged a good deal of the building but left the newly constructed service wing unscathed. Work then had to be started all over again, using Wyatt's structure as the core, as well as rescuing some of the surviving interiors.

Further alterations were then carried out around 1900 when the dining room was refitted and the stucco of the main block was renovated. The Bulkeleys remained in residence up until the outbreak of the First World War, and indeed returned briefly after the War's conclusion, but simply found such a huge house to be impractical. It was put up for sale in 1921 but failed to sell; it was subsequently advertised to be let but little interest was shown. The War Office requisitioned the mansion in WWII; it was only derequisitioned in 1948, following ten years of fires, vandalism and accidents. Despite being insured by the army, the extent of the damage was so great that the Bulkeleys were forced to shut down the house and grounds completely. Vandalism, theft and rot made the family consider demolition during the 1970s.

THE PROBLEM

What an astonishing house on an astonishing site, with surely some of the best views in Wales! But what a problem. This house is literally gargantuan and first became a real problem well before the First World War. Of course, it had been extended again and again in the days when staff were readily available at modest cost. Effectively, all of this stopped not far short of one hundred years ago, with the result that this wonderful example of cultivated architectural design genuinely had no sustainable use. It was therefore part of the list of horror stories in North Wales that included such other fine houses of size, such as Kinmel, Gwrych and Glynllifon. One can well feel sympathy for the owners who have been unable to find any form of solution, generation after generation. It is has simply been too big for any realistic use to have come to light so far.

FUTURE THOUGHTS AND POSSIBILITIES

On the face of it, this might be regarded as a hopeless case with no solution in sight. On the other hand, unlike many similar houses in Wales, options have been kept open by simply not going down the demolition route. Thus,

given the spectacular siting of this property, a theoretical conversion to residential use in multiple occupation could well spearhead a feasible rescue operation. Indeed, there would appear to be sufficient existing buildings on site to avoid the need for any significant additional enabling development. So, whilst the walls still stand there must always be the hope that someday something may be possible, especially in the light of recent increase in house prices. This is therefore very much a case of 'watch this space' – we wish all involved the best of luck in sorting this problem out.

BLAEN BAGLAN

House Listing Grade – II*
Authority – Neath Port Talbot

DESCRIPTION

Blaen Baglan, the ancient seat of the Williams', is situated near the head of a valley with phenomenal views towards the Gower Peninsula and Swansea Bay. The house was reconstructed in around 1600 by William Williams, who incorporated the core of his ancestor's earlier house. The male heirs had died out by the 1690s and the ownership of the estate thereafter is uncertain. By 1755, however, Blaen Baglan was leased or owned by the Davies family; during the early nineteenth century it formed part of the Jersey Estate as a tenanted farm.

Still part of a working farm, the house fell into disuse following the Second World War and a modern bungalow was subsequently constructed in the grounds nearby, though this too has now been abandoned. The front section of Blaen Baglan is essentially that of the 1600s house providing a hall and parlour on the ground floor; a rear wing was added in the mid-seventeenth century together with minor nineteenth century additions.

The Problem

As is obvious from the photograph, the primary problem is that the house is in a state of severe disrepair, although from a cursory inspection it did not appear to be caused by any fundamental structural problem. It was simply abandoned many years ago when a nearby bungalow was put up as alternative accommodation for the farm. Of course, the amount of work to bring this house around is likely to be considerable and, on the face of it Port Talbot, with its steel works, may not be considered an ideal setting by everyone. However, this particular site is generally a delight, with long views over the sea to the Gower Peninsula.

Future Thoughts and Possibilities

Given the will and determination to live in an ancient Welsh manor house with stunning views and the level of remoteness which provides high amenity, then, for the right person, Blaen Baglan is the answer to a prayer either for the present owner, or perhaps someone else. It certainly does not seem to be too large a house for single occupation, and should certainly fire the imagination and commitment of someone 'out there,' given that it is literally 'a bow-shot' away from the M4, with its quick access to Neath, Swansea, Port Talbot, Bridgend and Cardiff – how very lucky for the future occupant and their family!

BLAEN BLODAU

DESCRIPTION

Blaen Blodau, set among mature walled grounds in the very depths of lovely Cardiganshire, is an attractive early nineteenth century residence of some distinction. Little is known of its early history but, until 1890, it had belonged to the widowed Mrs Eliza Jones of Maesycrugiau. It was put up for sale first on 15th July 1902 and then again on 24th July 1906 together with about 1,100 acres consisting of thirty-five farms and various buildings. At this time, it was tenanted by Mr Frank Morgan, brother of Hugh Thomas Morgan, who died in 1893 at the age of twenty-five. The house was inhabited until fairly recently but is now in a poor state of repair; it is not dilapidated, as can be seen

from the illustrations. Some time ago, the owner instructed an architect to draw plans for restoration, but an application for grant aid was rejected. No work has been carried out since.

Built of two-storeys on a basement with two elliptical bows obscured by a Victorian or early twentieth century addition, the rear contains two similar bows with triple sash windows. Within the grounds is also a modest coach house dating from the mid-late nineteenth century. Despite being situated close to, but unaffected by, a working farm, the house is secluded enough to be a private home once again, despite being uninhabited for many years.

The Problem

The real problem here is that this delightful small house makes one's heart ache! This is because it is situated in a wonderful area, seemingly with more than enough ground and a small stable block nearby. Sadly, it seems to have been abandoned years ago and is now simply open to the winds. The grounds are very overgrown; the sunlight barely penetrates. Yet Blaen Blodau has lost none of its magic to appeal to the stranger who seeks it out. Certainly it is in need of repair and generally requires that kiss of life that only a caring and loving owner can bring. But surely there is no reason why this could not happen…tomorrow!

Future Thoughts and Possibilities

Given the modest size of the house, its delightful architecture, and its location in one of the most rural areas of Wales, there seems to be little problem at Blaen Blodau other than the will to 'make it happen.' Once this has been found, the property could again become a comfortable, cultivated family home within a matter of months. Let us hope that someone, somewhere, will care enough to ensure that this really does happen sooner rather than later.

BOVERTON PLACE

Scheduled Ancient Monument
House Listing Grade – II
Authority – Vale of Glamorgan County Council

DESCRIPTION

Built by Roger Seys towards the end of the sixteenth century, Boverton Place has been empty since the mid-nineteenth century. (Seys built it between 1591 and 1599 and was the Queen's Attorney to the Council in Wales and the Marches; he had married Elizabeth Voss, heiress of Boverton and a maid of honour to Queen Elizabeth I). The Seys family remained in occupation until the middle of the eighteenth century, when Boverton passed into the Fonmon estate, although a tourist from 1798 recorded that it had become 'a skeleton of an old mansion house.' It was still roofed in 1834, but, by the middle of the century, the house was stripped of all of its timbers, woodwork and decorative stonework for use as a neighbouring farmhouse. The mansion was essentially of three sections; the main storeyed range, the staircase tower and the parlour wing to the north. All of the

interior within the main range was wooden and has disappeared, but cellars remain under certain parts of the building. Despite its abandonment some one hundred and fifty years ago, the building is remarkably intact and is hugely impressive, perched high above Boverton village.

In April 2007, it was announced that Boverton was to be sold by auction with the guide price of £55,000 - £80,000, together with about an acre of land. Cadw stated that a sustainable reuse, where feasible, could present the best solution by which its future could be secured. In principle, Cadw say they would have no objections to the potential reuse of the building but planning permission from the Local Authority would of course be a prerequisite. It was subsequently sold at auction for about £70,000, although details of its future use have not yet been announced.

The Problem

Even a cursory visit to Boverton is a memorable experience on account of these magical ruins which are steeped in history. Sadly though, ruins is all we have here at the present time, but inevitably we shall lose even these if nothing is done to install a sustainable use within them. Clearly, there is no known intention for them to be consolidated as a picturesque architectural specimen, and indeed, the powers that be appear enlightened in their willingness to see the roof go back up and a beneficial use installed. However, it is a large building and reinstatement works are bound to be extensive; but what a glorious opportunity for the new owner.

Future Thoughts and Possibilities

Almost any future use will be better than to allow this wonderful piece of history to simply dismantle itself through rain, frost and general neglect. Sadly though, this is inevitable if nothing is done. On the other hand, the potential here is clearly enormous, and, with the right skills and approach, there is no reason why Boverton could not again become one of the great houses of South Wales and tomorrow's heritage. There is no reason why this process should not start with the reinstatement of part of the property and consolidation of the remainder pending further work being completed in years to come. In so many ways this house is similar to the challenges presented by countless Scottish castles in a similar condition that have nevertheless been brought back to life again over the past forty years or so as private houses. This could so easily happen here and we wish the new owners every good fortune for their stewardship of part of the national heritage and for their patronage of fine architecture.

A Case Study

House Listing Grade – NOT LISTED
Authority – Ceredigion County Council

DESCRIPTION

Bronwydd, the ancient seat of the Lloyds, was rebuilt for Thomas Davies Lloyd in 1853, by R. K. Penson along the lines of a Rhineland Castle, incorporating elements of the cathedral transept and tower of Rock Cashel, Ireland. Thomas Lloyd was created a baronet in 1863, befitting his new baronial mansion and social elevation. The estate of nearly eight thousand acres was inherited by his only son, Marteine, who went on to become High Sheriff of Cardiganshire in 1881 and a captain in the Pembrokeshire Yeoman Cavalry.

An Indian summer was felt at Bronwydd when a great ball was held to celebrate the golden wedding anniversary of Sir Marteine and Lady Lloyd in 1928. Sir Marteine died shortly afterwards at the age of eighty-two; he was the last baronet as his only son and heir had been killed in action at the Somme in 1916. A sale of contents followed and, in 1937, the Bronwydd estate of 2,072 acres was advertised for sale by auction in 98 lots. It is said that the sale of land close to the house for forestry work proved to be one of the final nails in the coffin for the future of the mansion. During the Second World War Bronwydd Castle, as it was then known, was Aryeh House School, a Jewish boarding school which ran successfully for several years. At the end of the War, the school returned to its original location at Hove.

Bronwydd was then sold on like many other houses in Wales to be stripped of its interior fixtures and fittings. However, the roof was still substantially intact and the house was believed rescuable even into the 1980s. This delicate situation was not to last and in recent years much of the surviving structure has been either demolished or collapsed. Today only the sturdy square end turret remains extant.

The Problem

This house perhaps more than most illustrates the fickle nature of human taste in architecture. Goodness, how the project captures the imagination of the builders; a large Victorian Gothic house of huge exuberance set in one of the most remote, bucolic and entrancing areas of Cardiganshire. The craftsmanship was as good as one can get, with exquisite attention to detail all linked to an almost juvenile romanticism. Although this did not last, and in reality it fell prey to changing tastes where such buildings were so easily labelled as a 'Victorian monstrosity.' Of course it never was such, although 'strong meat' it certainly it was.

Sad to say, this wonderful confection remained in existence well into the 1950s as a school. After that it really was redundant even though much of the roof was extant well into the 1980s. Since then (it was not listed,) it has gradually been demolished to the point that all that now remains are some walls and the main tower. What an utter shame for the Welsh countryside that we should now be denied this jewel of imagination when only twenty years ago something could have been done to keep options open.

Future Thoughts and Possibilities

The real trouble here is that most of the house has gone! But, at the time of our visit in the summer of 2007 at least one substantial tower remained. Let us hope that perhaps this small fragment of past glories could be converted to a holiday cottage akin to many of those so successfully rescued by the Landmark Trust. A thorough archaeological survey is desperately needed to record the remains of this illustrious mansion before what remains succumbs to the waiting bulldozer.

Brynglas Hall

House Listing Grade – II
Authority – Powys County Council

DESCRIPTION

A minor gentry house of seventeenth century origins, this house has been in poor condition for over twenty years. The rear of the property retains its seventeenth century appearance which includes timber windows and framing. Around 1800, a new front in the Regency style was added with projecting wings and gothic glazing, but the seventeenth century panelling and a staircase survived. One of the most intriguing features is the columned portico which is made out of wood and now has its capitals placed above the column on the pediment. Could this have been a vernacular interpretation of a classical design? Sold by auction at Welshpool on 13th August 1945, the house was described as having three reception rooms, six bedrooms, one bathroom together with a cottage, gardens and outbuildings; all set in eighty-three acres of land.

Today Brynglas is in a very sorry state; the roof is caving in, windows are smashed and structural problems are affecting the integrity of the structure. Some years ago to halt the collapse of the right hand gable, a dumper truck was placed against the wall to stop it bowing out! At the rear of this gable end a corner of the house has collapsed although there has been some attempt many years ago to prevent further damage.

The Problem

Anyone could be forgiven for thinking that there is not much hope here as the house appears to be demolishing itself. Part of the rear has actually come down and part of the front is clearly unstable. On the other hand it is not so bad as to warrant being written off as an entirely a 'no hope' This house really does reflect the patina of rural Wales, reflecting the aspirations of cultivated people wishing to be comfortable in a house of pleasing aesthetics in a delightful rural area. Yes, the structural problems are severe, but these are more than compensated for by its overall appeal and likely future amenity; at the right price, we would imagine that anything is possible.

Future Thoughts and Possibilities

In some ways the rescue of this good building has already begun, in that the worst structural defects have been temporarily stabilised with the dumper truck! The key to the future, however, depends upon the engagement of a skilled and pragmatic structural engineer who really does know the intimacies of traditional buildings, so that a whole range of structural solutions may be considered in order to save the house economically. Surely, there is no doubt that this is possible on the basis of 'where there is a will there is a way.' It will then provide the lucky owner with a home of generous proportions satisfying architectural innovation and comfortable aesthetics. Add to this a delightful location in one of the most unspoilt areas of rural Wales (sometimes referred to as the Welsh Tuscany) and one really could have a 'magical mix.' It is to be hoped that there is somebody out there who yearns for this combination sufficiently strongly.

A Case Study

House Listing Grade – NOT LISTED
Authority – Gwynedd County Council

DESCRIPTION

Forlorn Brynkir, this historic pile was once approached by a carriage drive bordered with magnificent beech trees, but today the house stands in ruins. It had been built in the beautiful Pennant Valley amidst the dramatic scenery of the Llyn Peninsula, close to the remains of an old mansion. The new Brynkir had been substantially built of dressed local stone of the highest quality with fashionable canted and bowed bays and galleried wings. Parts date from the seventeenth century with major additions in the late eighteenth and nineteenth centuries.

Captain Joesph Huddart, an influential sea captain, inventor, chartmaker, and entrepreneur,

purchased the ancient demesne of Brynkir in 1809 and, over the proceeding two years, added greatly to the estate. His invention of a rope-making device, patented in 1793, grossed the fortune which enabled him to purchase the estate. Huddart's son received a knighthood from King George IV in 1821. On his death, the estate passed to his eldest son, George Augustus Huddart, one of eight children. George saw himself as an inventor like his grandfather but he failed to find acclaim for any of his inventions. His heavy mortgaging of the estate (which rose to over £60,000 during the mid-nineteenth century) plunged both estate and family into dire debt. So much so that, by the time of his death in

1885, the estate was forced to be administered by the Court of Chancery, which arranged various sales to pay off outstanding debts.

A certain Richard Greaves purchased the core of the estate from the Trustees of George Augustus Huddart in 1903 when it became a principal residence again. Various events were held there including tea parties, sports days and luncheons. During the First World War, Brynkir was used to house German Prisoners of War: indeed, various stories have survived which record how when the prisoners had gone for a walk one day and not returned on time, a panic spread amongst the populace locally. One other story tells of soldiers breaking into Mr Greave's wine cellar and emptying the contents! Brynkir Camp finally closed on 29th October 1919 when the prisoners were transferred to Frongoch on the 5.51am train.

In 1930, the last owner to reside in the mansion moved out and the estate was put up for sale. Brynkir's structure was said to be generally in good condition, but prospective purchasers were advised that by 'taking down the more modern parts and back wings the residence could be made more suitable for present day requirements.' Entry to the house was through a multi-storeyed porch of mid-nineteenth century date into a large entrance hall off which opened the dining room, drawing room, morning room and staircase hall. The staircase and screen were noted to be very fine and made out of pitch pine, being all in excellent condition in 1930. Bedroom accommodation was commodious, totalling some sixteen rooms in all over the first and second floors – not so large if one considers half this number to be dressing rooms, serving bedrooms.

Within the succeeding fifteen years the house was sold and the building stripped of its fixtures and fittings. All windows, floors, doors, roofs and ceilings were removed; the grounds were stripped of their ornamental planting and the skeletal ruins were left open to the elements.

THE PROBLEM

This property raises a whole gamut of conflicting emotion; utter dismay with photographs showing a fine building and a ruin and quick succession, indifference to some of the bad architectural elements, joy from a gloriously located site, and admiration for huge quantities of finely cut granite building blocks. Indeed, although in some way this house is a mess of differing styles and quality, it certainly has huge potential to be rationalise into a coherent mansion of the highest craft quality. But who is the owner? Nobody knows! This place has been in limbo for generations.

FUTURE THOUGHTS AND POSSIBILITIES

Although enormous, at present Brynkir looks pretty derelict. Yet an astonishing opportunity nevertheless remains here for the site to be reused as a distinguished home. Large parts of the main walls exist in fine-dressed stone with much good detailing surviving. Thus, there are wide options as to whether the granite can be used as it is, or in some remodelled form, but what a waste for nothing to be happening. It could so easily bring large funds, jobs and fine craftsmanship back into this sparsely populated area of the highest amenity value.

Bwlch-Mawr

House Listing Grade – II
Authority – Powys County Council

Description

One of the most amazing sights for a conservationist! This late-medieval timber framed hall house was converted to a storeyed house circa 1600 has been preserved by a caring farmer who did not wish to see his family home demolished when it had become redundant, even though it was in the way of farming activities. Bwlch Mawr has been uninhabited since 1966, when the new farmhouse was built a few yards away. Since then, a new farm building has actually been built over the old farmhouse, thus preventing any serious decay. This remarkable survivor still retains some original furniture and fittings from the time the family transferred to the modern house.

Bwlch Mawr seems to have been remodelled in the early eighteenth century when a central entrance was inserted; a date of 1712 is inscribed on a window jamb. An early nineteenth century stable was demolished when the barn was constructed over the house. Nonetheless, Bwlch Mawr is a delightful example of a Welsh vernacular farm house which has survived unaltered through the centuries. Parts of the house are in still in use for storage but some work is needed to conserve the fabric in the long run.

The Problem

One can well understand that, due to its structural condition, layout and size that this utterly charming house was not considered to be suitable as a farm house for the latter part of the twentieth century and beyond. But what great ingenuity and resilience was demonstrated by the owner having the best of both worlds in this instance; he now has his family home and his cattle shed with one inside the other! Nevertheless, the underlying problem remains in that the old house is unsuitable as a farm house, especially as a comfortable new dwelling has now been built only a few feet away. Thus the problem is somewhat intractable as the building is redundant as a farmhouse, yet is not deteriorating significantly at present under the cover of a modern farm building.

Future Thoughts and Possibilities

It seems there is no more viable a solution here other than routine repairs and 'leave well alone.' Someday, perhaps, the old house could be conserved (as found) as a visitors attraction if the owners wished to go down this route or maybe the most unusual holiday cottage. Otherwise there appears not to be the need to do much more than has already been done, other than routine maintenance.

House Listing Grade – II*
Authority – Cardiff City Council

DESCRIPTION

Built as offices for the Taff Vale Railway, and first used in 1843, but the southern section was apparently an addition of the 1860s. Following construction of new offices at Queen St in 1862, the building was let as a consulate (and known as 'Consulate Chambers'), but with a waiting room and ticket office in southern section. It's original name was the Cardiff Docks Station. Adapted as a regular station in the early twentieth century, following the closure of the old Cardiff Docks Station, it is still a fine building as proven by its listing.

In 1925, a platform and canopy was added to improve conditions for commuters. Following a restoration in the 1980s, the old station was used by the National Museums and Galleries of Wales and the Butetown Historical Railway Society as a railway museum, prior to its closure in 1997. The premises are at the time of writing being offered to let and planning permission has been granted for conversion to a bar and restaurant. Now with holes in the roof, windows smashed and a collapsing interior, work is urgently needed to be carried out on site. Its recent neglect is not a matter of pride for any of us in the conservation movement.

THE PROBLEM

This building could not be more central to the industrial history of South Wales and how fortunate we are that it has survived at all, let alone in its relatively good state as a shell to this present day. If there is a real problem here it is that no-one of late has had the inspiration to go ahead and convert it for some form of beneficial use – use as a bar/restaurant seems as good as any.

FUTURE THOUGHTS AND POSSIBILITIES

Even in its somewhat tired and dilapidated state, this is a keynote building (opposite the National Assembly) in a keynote area (Cardiff Bay) in a keynote city that continues to reinvent itself. Here, surely, is a worthwhile opportunity for an enlightened developer to make the most of both the building, its location and its history through a sensitive and sympathetic conversion. Conservationists must avoid the risk of asking for too much of a developer and possibly losing the building entirely as a result.

House Listing Grade – II*
Authority – Cardiff City Council

DESCRIPTION

The Cardiff Exchange Building fills the entire centre of Mount Stuart Square and was built in 1884-86 to the design of Edwin Seward of Seward & Thomas Architects, on site of the central gardens to house the administration of the coal exchange. Constructed in the French Renaissance style of Bath stone on a Pennant stone plinth, the later west section was built in yellow brick with Bath stone and corner dressings. This vast building once provided offices for all manner of businesses connected with the coal and shipping trade, while the Coal Exchange Hall itself accommodated a stock exchange for the shipping and coal trades of South Wales. Indeed, Barclays Bank has occupied the north-east corner since the Exchange first opened.

Further extensions were added in 1893, with the north wing being completed in 1897. It was at this time that the new additions departed from Seward's original plans, omitting elements such as domed corner roof turrets. Interior alterations to the Exchange Hall were carried out by Seward again in 1911-12, but in the 1970s a false ceiling was inserted in the Exchange Hall itself which has hidden the upper level gallery and roof trusses. This was accompanied by the addition of a highly unsympathetic and visually damaging underground car park which disfigured the main entrance.

Since trading ceased in 1961, much of the building has been effectively vacant; thus both internally and externally it has suffered from inadequate maintenance and security. Fire gutted the east wing, destroying the main staircase to the upper floors, leaving this part of the buildings an empty and derelict shell. Water ingress together with extensive dry rot has ravaged vast parts of the structure. Scaffolding supports the burnt out shell of the east wing and Barclays

Bank has recently vacated the ground floor due to the poor condition of this section of the Exchange. Efforts have been made to address the problems but due to the complicated roof structures and expanse, this has not been an easy task. Proposals have been recently put forward to restore the main hall and to remedy the later alterations with demolition. Importantly, it has been proposed that the concrete parking bunker could be removed. Planning permission, with an application for listed building consent, was submitted and a public inquiry followed. In March of 2008 it was announced that the Inspector had recommended that consent for the application to be granted, subject to conditions.

The Problem

Is it really such a problem that this building which was put up at the height of coal mining prosperity when Welsh steam coal was exported all over the world has not yet found a sustainable new use? The Welsh Coal traded here facilitated many industrial revolutions in countless countries abroad whilst at the same time oiling the wheels of empire by facilitating cheap transportation of its commercial goods? In some ways, therefore, this building is of international importance; this is where most of the world's coal was traded amongst brokers, mining companies, shippers and end users. This is precisely the time when the Royal Navy actually did rule the waves; most of their ships were powered by Welsh coal. The grandeur of this building therefore fully reflects its international significance. Sadly, it has not been in full use or properly maintained for some time.

Future Thoughts and Possibilities

Of course, a building of this size and style is bound periodically to require a major overhaul. Thus it is not surprising that it is now shabby and in some disrepair, but these small drawbacks fade into oblivion when one considers the potential grandeur of the accommodation not only in itself and its location but as an ongoing illustration of Wales reinventing itself. It could not be in that much of a better location, but again as with other buildings in South Wales it needs just that one organisation eager enough to commit their own future for a time to the survival of this great cultural asset.

Carmarthen Guildhall, Carmarthen

Building Listing Grade – I
Authority – Carmarthenshire

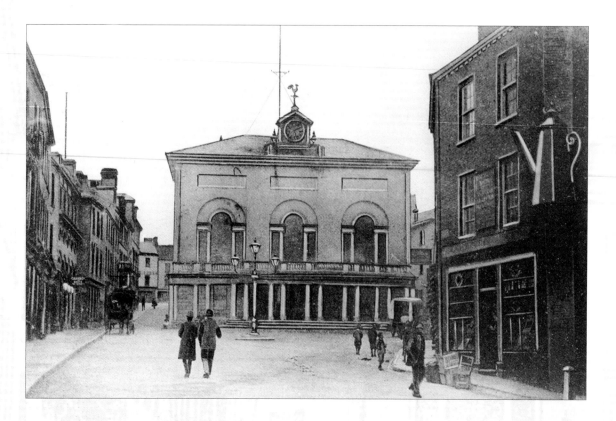

Description

Designed in 1767 by Sir Robert Taylor, who may have used the Guildhall as a 'trial-run' for the Bank of England design in London. Completion took ten years as the funds were not forthcoming immediately. Further rooms and alterations were carried out by a local architect, Thomas Humphreys in about 1780 and in 1811 a curved double staircase was added to the front. More Victorian alterations took place and in 1910 the Court Room was redecorated and fitted up in the Edwardian style. However, the exterior was radically altered by the removal of the render in the mid-twentieth century.

Owned by the County Council, it was transferred to the Lord Chancellor's Department on April 1st 2005 who then proceeded to put it on the open market but thankfully, following public pressure it was purchased by the County Council who have not yet found a suitable use as of yet.

STOP PRESS! The building continues in use as the Crown Court.

The Problem

This is a great building and an ornament to any shire town. On the other hand, it is fragile and needs a sensitive and enlightened hand, even for day-to-day care and maintenance. The problem appears to be one of lack of perceived beneficial use, yet it is in the very centre of Carmarthen. One thing is for sure: irrespective of cost, this building must never be lost. It represents far too much of our own identity as Welsh people as well as those worthy citizens of Carmarthen.

Future Thoughts and Possibilities

Obviously the ultimate future use of this building must be for the people of Carmarthen to decide, however there are ample examples up and down the country where such buildings have been opened to the public, to be used as concert halls, museums, tea room, restaurants and a plethora of other uses. Given the strong commitment there appears to be locally for keeping this building within community use, then innovative ideas should abound from local consultation. In the meantime a full program of repairs should be commenced as whatever the use this building, it will remain public property, or so it seems. Nevertheless the current use as the Crown Court seems ideal and hopefully may continue despite recent uncertainty.

House Listing Grade – II*
Authority – Ceredigion County Council

DESCRIPTION

Situated within the stately ruins of Cardigan Castle, Castle Green House festers slowly as the river Teifi flows by. John Bowen began the first house on site in 1808, using the foundations of the thirteenth century Great Tower as its own. Castle Green was further extended in 1827 for the High Sheriff, Arthur Jones. The architect was David Evans who incorporated a circular thirteenth century tower to the rear, which originally formed part of the castle. Another High Sheriff, David Davies, purchased the house in 1836 and proceeded to make further alterations. After nearly one hundred years

of occupation, the Davies' family sold Castle Green and purchased Plas Llangoedmor, Cardiganshire instead. A local auctioneer then lived in the house until it passed to Mrs Barbara Woods in 1940.

Due to years of neglect and vandalism, by the late 1990s the house was in a perilous condition. Ceredigion Council procured the site in 2003 for £500,000 with a vision for opening it as a tourist attraction for Cardigan. In 2004, it was one of the top eight finalists competing in the BBC's Restoration series. Castle Green House has been recently subject to a feasibility study to ascertain potential, economically viable, end-uses. Today, the house has been made weather tight whilst an end use continues to be sought.

The Problem

Essentially, the problem here stems from a long term lack of maintenance which has resulted in this very fine house becoming ruinous and uninhabitable. Yet it is part of the iconic Cardigan Castle and one cannot but admire the determination of the people of Cardigan to acquire this whole complex and thus take control over their own history. It is truly heartening to come across such determination against all the odds by people who really care. Indeed it reminds one of Goethe's comment to the effect that those who value their inheritance should earn it again if they really are to possess it. The worthy citizens of Cardigan are certainly doing this, despite the fact that funding is a headache and no really sustainable use has yet been identified.

Future Thoughts and Possibilities

In some ways the problem has been solved simply by way of the people of Cardigan feeling so strongly about their heritage that they have bought this building back against the odds. By covering the house with a temporary roof, they have allowed time to identify a sustainable long term solution as to users and funding. One hopes, therefore, that a solution can be found whereby part of the property can be used commercially in some way or another in order to pay for general running costs of those areas that will be open to the public. But, hopefully never again will this important piece of Welsh heritage get into the pickle it has been in until quite recently.

Building Listing Grade – II
Authority – Cardiff City Council

DESCRIPTION

On the 10th July 1859 the first burial took place at the newly opened cemetery in Cathays. The chapels were built during the same year to the designs of R.G. Thomas of Newport and Thomas Waring of Cardiff, at a cost of £5,200. At a glance, the chapels look identical, yet on closer inspection the right hand building is the more ornate of the two and was used for Episcopal denominations such as the Church in Wales. Conversely, the left hand chapel was unconsecrated and served for Non-conformist services and burials.

A pair of porte-cochères provided covered entrances into the twin chapels to shelter the horse-drawn hearses whilst the coffin was transferred inside. The central bell tower's roof was originally taller and more imposing, yet it is still commanding over this tranquil area of Cardiff. One of Cardiff's many Gothic buildings, these chapels are stone faced and roofed with Welsh slates. Since closing in 1992, there have been measures to prevent further deterioration of the internal fabric with temporary roofing being put over both chapels and all windows and doors have been blocked. Additionally, the building has been surrounded by a metal fence which looks horrid but perhaps keep the vandals at bay. The cemetery is locked up every evening, which also helps.

The Problem

How strange it is that the cause of the current problem is precisely the same as the need for the building in the first instance: 'life after death.' Here we have some really fine architecture that is unlikely ever to be repeated again for stylistic, cultural and financial reasons and yet here it is redundant for its original use, unloved and unmaintained. In spite of this, it is virtually in the centre of Cardiff. The central problem therefore could be little more than the need to put the building on the market at a nominal figure to encourage lateral thinkers with a penchant for gothic architecture of the nineteenth century to come up with a viable alternative use.

Future Thoughts and Possibilities

This wonderful quirky building is situated just off Cardiff city centre in a mainstream residential area. Surely, a public use could be found that serves the adjacent community and yet is still in sympathy with its immediate surroundings as a cemetery and to those who visit. Cadw states that this is in fact Wales' finest public cemetery building, yet what should be one of Cardiff's prime assets is a blight in the centre of the cemetery which, in itself, is beautifully kept and frequently visited. It seems astonishing that even providing some sort of sustenance and shelter for the cemetery's visitors has not been created in this wonderful building. Let us hope the ingenuity of 'Joe Public' can be tapped to find a solution by widely marketing it for whatever reasonable figure precipitates a new use; it is after all an area where the finer feelings of mankind abound.

House Listing Grade – II*
Authority – Powys County Council

DESCRIPTION

Cefn Bryntalch dates from 1869 . Designed by G. F. Bodley, it has been regarded as the start of the Georgian Revival of the 1870s. It is interesting to note that when Bodley fell ill, Philip Webb was asked to complete the project. This is one of the most well preserved examples of Bodley's domestic architecture and shows how a late Victorian house could be created with remarkable refinement. It was built for Richard Edward Jones, whose fortune had been made in the flannel trade. His descendants lived at the house for several generations. One of its more famous inhabitants was the composer Peter Warlock, who lived there intermittently from 1903 until his death in 1930. It was here that most of his music was composed.

The design of the house is skilful in its fusion of vernacular architecture with that of early Georgian revival. The building is constructed of red brick under tiled roofs; to the rear of which is a small courtyard containing service buildings. Today, the house is on the market after various people fought off some rogue planning applications for development close by. This could be a most gorgeous private house set within its own grounds – certainly it has a very distinguished pedigree.

The Problem

Oh dear! How this house, high up on a hill not far from Welshpool, has mirrored the fate of Welsh country houses all too closely. It is not so big as to have been emptied of human life, but it does now need the usual hundred-year overhaul which all buildings need from time to time. This is especially so with regard to its extensive range of outbuildings. So, essentially, the problem is little more than a backlog of repair, to be undertaken by a committed new owner. Once done, the property would fully deserve the description of one of Wales's domestic icons.

Future Thoughts and Possibilities

Here again we have an architectural gem on a wonderful site in a delightful, unspoilt rural location. There is no fundamental reason why this should not change hands without trouble as a private dwelling of much distinction. It has recently been on the market and is just sitting there waiting for an inspired new owner's commitment to make it again one of the foremost family houses in the area. Alternatively, the property would make a fine B&B location or even a small hotel with holiday cottages in the buildings, although use as a private residence is probably best.

CILWENDEG PIGEON HOUSE AND STABLES

House Listing Grade – II*
Authority –Pembrokeshire County Council

DESCRIPTION

Cilwendeg itself was built mostly during the late eighteenth century; the name translates as 'fair white nook.' The appearance of the building has not departed considerably from its nineteenth century state, consisting of three floors and two wings which stand at two storeys high. At either side of these wings is a pair of Victorian conservatories; the house is used as an old people's home under the auspices of Pembrokeshire County Council.

The pigeon and poultry house was built circa 1835 for Morgan Jones the second; to a degree of elaboration unparalleled in Wales, the ground floor wings were said to have been built for ducks and geese, whilst turkeys were housed in the central section with dogs in the connecting parts. Hens were kept on the first floor and pigeons on the upper shelves; utterly remarkable. It is a gem, even though it is in need of repair.

52

The Problem

This was and perhaps still is one of the great estates of Wales; originally it derived its huge income from The Skerries lighthouse in the nineteenth century. As may be expected, therefore, the estate is peppered with delightful buildings including the delectable shell house and a rare survival of a specially-built pigeon house amongst other things. The bow-fronted stable in particular is something of an eye-catcher, but the problem is this: the house is not of huge proportions and is currently in institutional use as a county council care home separate from the remainder of the estate. Thus, this use may be little more than a temporary expedient in practise. So often we have seen properties in this situation being marketed ineffectively through commercial agents, unloved and unwanted, and thus at grave risk of being lost like Pant Glas. This scenario could well be on the cards at some time in the future.

Future Thoughts and Possibilities

In theory there is no reason why this great estate should not again be reunited under one ownership, but who could make this possible we wonder. Certainly the house with its gardens remaining pretty well untouched, is a delight with its pair of matching conservatories, one on each side of the garden elevation. Add to that the core of an eighteenth century house and a sandstone porte-cochere, and it could with enthusiasm become a stunning home once again someday. This may then provide the means for a unified ownership and the rescue of the various amenity buildings on the estate. This property cries out for a person of ingenuity, dedication, resilience and with sufficient funding, but there is no fundamental reason why the main house at Cilwendeg should not again flourish as one of Wales's great estates. Let us hope that someone will come up with significant grant aid to secure the future of the Pigeon House.

Listing Grade – I
Authority – Pembrokeshire County Council

Description

Built on a pre-Norman site, the present St. Daniels may incorporate twelfth century fabric, but it was enlarged in the later medieval period. The tower dates from the fourteenth or fifteenth century but with later alterations. During the eighteenth century, the church was used as a dissenting chapel by the Reverend Howell Davies, Moderator of the Calvinists of Pembrokeshire, and also by John Wesley, who preached here during the late 1760s and early 1770s.

St. Daniels consists of nave, chancel, and west tower which have internally pointed vaulted roofs. Pembrokeshire County Council have stated in the past that this building does not lend itself very well to a permanent residential conversion, but it could potentially find a use as a holiday let. St. Daniels has only recently been sold to a lay owner who has made the building wind and water tight, yet it still remains one of the county buildings at risk. It is not known what current plans are in store for this stark and rugged church to be rescued by way of a viable future use.

The Problem

This is just the sort of church that makes the grain and character of our countryside so fascinating and beautiful. Isolated in the lovely Pembrokeshire, it is redolent of a God-fearing rural community that has 'ploughed the fields and scattered' for thousands of years.

It demonstrates more ably than any words the fortitude, faith and dedication of our Christian forbears who built it and who now seem so separate from us ideologically that they could be on another planet. How sad, therefore, that this lovely landmark should be at risk. We can do no more than to wish the current owners well with the job of seeing this fine building into the twenty-first century. This is certainly not an easy task on account of the design and nature of the building which restricts wider possibilities of conversion and alteration. One cannot help wondering whether every effort was made to keep this delightful little church in some form of religious or community use. It seems so sad that its original use after many hundreds of years actually has now come to an end.

Future Thoughts and Possibilities

Now is the time to spare no effort in finding a new use for this church that will doubtlessly involve innovative and original architectural solutions, very probably for some form of residential use. A certain amount of compromise will be inevitable, if this building is to survive more or less intact. It is to be hoped that, if this proves to be impossible, then both local and wider community use of some form should be possible. One thing is for sure; that good first aid repairs and maintenance will be vital during the time that the building's future is being worked out, to secure the fabric from further deterioration.

Edwinsford, Talley

House Listing Grade – II*
Gardens Listing Grade – II (including Grade II bridge)
Authority – Carmarthenshire

Description

Edwinsford is serenely situated on the banks of the River Cothi in a Valley of the same name. The river separates the house from its service buildings, over which crosses an elegant single arched bridge. In about 1635 a square house with a large central chimney and pyramidal stone-clad roof was constructed. During the late seventeenth century, the central section was built or re-built for Sir Rice Williams, High Sheriff of Carmarthenshire in 1680. Another wing was added in 1842 at the back of house to contain the dining room and service section; the central section's main façade was remodelled for Sir James Hamlyn Williams possibly to the design of Edward Haycock. Twenty years later, in 1862, a French Renaissance wing to the right of the central block was erected to house the drawing room or ballroom on the site of a former chapel. One of the principal features of the interiors was

the fine plaster ceilings which were carefully recorded by the Royal Commission before they fell to the ground. Thankfully, the open-well staircase has been saved and is in full use at a private house near to Llandovery.

Following a family rift in the twentieth century, the estate was left to the butler after the death of Sir James Hamlyn Williams-Drummond in 1970; since then there have been several changes of ownership. One owner stripped the lead and slates off the roof and then sold most of the internal fittings without any official hindrance. Today, the roof has completely gone from the central block and 1862 wing, whilst the earliest section of the house remains partially roofed, albeit perilously so. Current planning legislation may as well not have existed, for all the protection that Edwinsford missed.

Around the house itself are the remains of a charming pleasure garden that sat on the land to the north, west and east of the mansion. Before World War Two some of the gate pillars were topped with painted lead figures. Cadw states that this owed more to the Gardenesque style rather than the High Victorian. Today, all of this has relapsed to rough grass and self-seeded saplings. The gardens and parkland occupy the undulating ground of the Cothi Valley, stretching over many acres.

The Problem

Some thirty years ago, one of the co-authors of this book travelled up to Hawthornden Castle, just outside of Edinburgh, to meet with the family Butler to discuss the future of the house, which could then be inspected room by room. What was deeply moving was to be shown an ink-well, constructed from the hoof of the last ox to plough the land at Edwinsford. Certainly the entrance hall and adjoining passages were very derelict at that time due to the lead having been stolen off the flat roofs, but generally the house was in remarkable good order even to the extent of some of the furniture remaining in situ. Sadly, no headway was made with the butler

and the dereliction continued unabated. This accelerated when, as indicated, a new owner decided to strip the house of its salvageable materials. Seemingly and inexplicably, no authority was inclined to stop this from happening.

Future Thoughts and Possibilities

Lovely, delectable and magical Edwinsford is now so ruined as to make one weep. But, there is plenty remaining to form the basis of a new house incorporating what remains. This would indeed be a formidable challenge, but for someone who is familiar with the building industry and is capable of getting the work done themselves, perhaps by employing direct labour, then this property could be the opportunity of a century. Certainly, with a little luck, there is the chance for these crumbling walls to see something of a renaissance. In doing so, the owner would acquire a home in one of the loveliest rural areas of the Principality with a remarkable, delightful history and the highest level of amenity. The views are exquisite. The total outlay could well be less than the cost of buying a four-bedroomed house in Datchet, if an owner is really determined.

Faenol Old Hall Listing Grade – I
Gardens Listing Grade – I
Authority – Gwynedd County Council

DESCRIPTION

Faenol Old Hall lies at the centre of the ancient manor or Maenol close to the university city of Bangor. During the Medieval period, Faenol was in the hands of the Bishops of Bangor until it was given to the Cochwillan family in 1533. By marriage, they became the Williams of Faenol with a baronetcy created in 1608. The estate left the Williams family ownership when it reverted to the Crown after the last member of the family died without issue in 1696. John Smith MP, Chancellor of the Exchequer and speaker of the House of Commons, was then granted the estate by 1723; in 1764 it was willed to Thomas Ashehton of Cheshire (a distant relation) who then assumed the name Smith as well. Through

the marriages of various descendants the names of Duff and Vivian were introduced. The estate was then enlarged enormously from the wealth created from the Dinorwic Slate Quarries. Thus the family frequently entertained royalty on their visits to Wales. Up until 1980 the family continued in residence; the estate was subsequently sold off in small portions in 1984, following the death of Sir Michael Duff, the last hereditary owner.

Faenol Old Hall, which is part of the estate buildings, dates to the first half of the sixteenth century. It was enlarged during the first half of the seventeenth century; the rear stair wing is dated on close-studding to 1638. Cadw states that this grade 1 listed building is an outstanding house of largely sixteenth century date, together with an exceptionally well-preserved main front and an interior of special interest. Also Grade I listed is Faenol New Hall, which replaced an earlier house as the principal residence on the estate. It dates to the late eighteenth-century (it does not appear on the estate of the 1770s) but was extensively remodelled in the nineteenth century, principally by Thomas Assheton Smith in 1825. Twentieth century alterations took place in 1901-5 and in 1912, but in 1959 a wing was demolished by Clough Williams Ellis, and a new classical entrance hall created in its place.

The Problem

On the face of it, there is no great problem here, as a grade one listed building. Faenol Old Hall is of course a remarkable survivor as the former principal house of this great estate, yet sadly it is not in beneficial use and at the time of inspection was neither wind nor water tight. On the other hand, as far as one can tell, there is no catastrophic disrepair problem here even though the house is derelict. This remarkable estate has over forty listed buildings at its core.

Future Thoughts and Possibilities

With a skilled conservation rescue programme, this notable house could once again become a family home of utmost distinction. The gardens, until quite recently, were considered to be some of the most notable in the area and could thus be rescued without great difficulty. Certainly this house is not too large to become a family home again: it seems curious that this has not already happened. It could therefore be a wonderful opportunity for the right person at the right time. The Old Hall in particular is crying out for a new resident owner.

House Listing Grade – II*

Authority – Pembrokeshire County Council

Description

Dating from 1794, Foley House is Haverfordwest's only example of the work of John Nash, and is unquestionably the most important residential building in the town. It was designed by Nash towards the end of his sojourn in Wales, for one Richard Foley whose country house, Ridgeway, lies some half-dozen miles to the east. Richard Foley was the elder brother of Captain Thomas Foley, later Admiral Sir Thomas, one of Nelson's most distinguished subordinates, and the naval hero himself is known to have visited Foley House. The building is almost identical in plan to Priory House in Cardigan, although in this case the exterior is classical in style. Internally it reflects Nash's liking (which he shared with his mentor Sir Robert Taylor) for rooms of somewhat unusual shape. On the ground floor were, besides the entrance hall, a drawing room with large bay windows, dining room, smoking room and cloakroom; while on the first floor were four large bedrooms, plus dressing rooms. Additional accommodation was contained in the basement.

Foley House remained in private ownership until after World War Two, by which time it was standing empty and neglected. In 1947 it was bought by Haverfordwest Borough Council, whose motive was, at least in part, to preserve it from further deterioration. In the immediate post-war period, of course, there was virtually no demand for houses of this size and type. Unhappily the Local Authority later made the mistake of supplanting Nash's stuccowork, which had been showing signs of wear, with wholly inappropriate roughcast which survives to this day. In the decades that followed, the house provided meeting rooms for council committees and offices for council employees.

The Problem

As a result of local government reorganization, ownership of the property eventually passed to Pembrokeshire County Council which has evidently had some difficulty in deciding what to do with it. The garden entrance allows limited parking for the privileged few, but the house itself is empty, shabby and deteriorating. Sadly, this enchanting villa demonstrates, all too clearly, that institutional use and architectural distinction rarely make a happy marriage.

Future Thoughts and Possibilities

At present the building needs a thorough conservation overhaul, which would not be cheap and would surely be best facilitated by a reversion to residential use. One option for the County Council, therefore, would be to put this fine house up for sale to a private buyer. It occupies a splendid site, above an ample garden that slopes away towards the High Street, affording views over the town and towards the castle on the opposite hillside. Given appropriate marketing, it could provide the Council with something of a windfall, and the new owner with the opportunity of a lifetime in recreating a family home of great distinction. Regrettably, this is not an option that the Council seems likely to adopt. Having first rejected a plan that would lead to the garden becoming part of a terraced car park for the benefit of occupants of properties in the High Street, the Council has now reversed that decision, and given the car park the go-ahead. That the garden should be removed in favour of someone else's car park would naturally reduce the appeal of Foley House to any prospective purchaser. In any case, it seems that building is destined become Haverfordwest's new Registry Office, where marriages will be conducted, and brides photographed against a John Nash backdrop. That will no doubt serve to keep the building standing, although it may not eliminate the aforementioned problems associated with institutional use.

Fort Hubberston, Milford Haven

Scheduled Ancient Monument
Building Listing Grade – II*
Authority – Pembrokeshire County Council

Description

Constructed at the request of Lord Palmerston between 1860 and 1865 at a reputed cost of £87,894, Fort Hubberston is perhaps one of the most impressive of the forts built along Milford Haven. It was originally intended to house twelve heavy guns in the battery, with seven others nearby and a garrison of some two hundred and fifty men in the barracks. Built of blue-rock limestone and laid with remarkable precision, the roofs are brick vaulted and of excellent quality.

Though abandoned in 1908 following no real hostilities, the fort was used in both the first and second World Wars for troop accommodation. During October 1932, the fort was sold by the Crown for £1,050 at a Swansea auction. Today the site is badly vandalized and almost wholly derelict. It must be emphasised that Fort Hubberston forms part of a highly sophisticated defensive network which in Britain is only comparable elsewhere with the defences on the Solent.

The Problem

The problem here is that Napoleon III is dead! Thus this fort and many others like it in the area are redundant and have been for a very long time. On the other hand, it is superbly built, but of gargantuan size, with massive constructional detail. Nevertheless, it is a delightful example of Victorian military architecture which could in fact survive for a very long time without intervention. But what a waste for this huge building on the edge of the Haven, with its remarkable views, to be allowed to fester.

Future Thoughts and Possibilities

Given the depressing state of property supply nationwide, let alone in Pembrokeshire, surely there is great potential here for ongoing residential conversion. Perhaps with a multi-use commercial future, but one will never know without this property actually being put on the market for sale as widely as possible with an appropriate planning brief as to what use the county council will allow. This is all it takes to tap into the dynamism and inventiveness of an enthusiastic developer. Let us hope that somebody soon sees this fort for what it is; a considerable asset, locked away in the mists of time. It could and should be actively serving the local community.

Fort Listing Grade – II*
Authority – Gwynedd County Council

DESCRIPTION

A rare and remarkable example of an eighteenth century folly fortification, forming a key although detached part of the impressive pleasure gardens of the Glynllifon Estate, Fort Williamsburg was built in 1761 by Sir Thomas Wynn following his election as MP for Caernarvonshire and his appointment as Constable of Caernarvon Castle and Lord Lieutenant, which made him responsible for the county's militia. A noted eccentric, he obsessively followed these responsibilities with zeal, constructing his own private garrison within the park at Glynllifon.

To commemorate the coronation of King George III, Sir Thomas founded the garrison at Fort Williamsburg together with a sisterhood and a volunteer organisation. The intention was for the garrison to comprise a Commander-in-Chief, a Governor, Lieutenant-Governor, one hundred officers, an Archdeacon, twenty-four chaplains, twenty-four honorary members and an unlimited number of volunteers. At the expense of Sir Thomas, all of the officers wore full and colourful uniforms. They were mobilised for a year whilst there was a threat of French invasion, although even after the Treaty of Paris in 1763 the garrison continued to meet. However, with the threat of the American War of Independence, Sir Thomas turned his attentions to constructing a new defensive sea-facing structure at Fort Belan. This did not stop work at Fort Williamsburg; the Tower was constructed between 1773–6 and a gatehouse and armoury were constructed in the Neo-classical style during the 1830s, reflecting the rebuilding of the main house. The most notable structure within the fort is the orangery with its cottage to the rear.

The Problem

This property is no less than a piece of heaven on earth. The tower is within the earth boundary of the fort which could some day so easily become a garden of great distinction. One can understand the reluctance of the former hereditary owners not wishing to sell off such a jewel in the centre of their land holding. On the other hand, that time has now passed and, unless some use of it is made, inevitably it will be lost to future generations, which would be unconscionable.

Future Thoughts and Possibilities

Surely the ideal solution here is for the armoury, orangery and barracks/cottages to the rear to be treated as one, perhaps with some inconsequential extension which could create a house of great amenity overlooking the centre of the fort with the tower as an eye-catcher, possibly even containing guest accommodation. The additional opportunity to create one of the great gardens of Wales is obvious. One just hopes that those in authority here at Glynllifon could bring themselves to grasp the nettle not only to ensure that the fort is saved for posterity, but also perhaps to ensure that it is available for the public enjoyment on occasion. The potential here for all concerned to derive great benefit from our common heritage is endless.

Foxhall Newydd

Scheduled Ancient Monument
House Listing Grade – I
Dovecote – II
Gardens Listing Grade – II
Authority – Denbighshire

Description

Foxhall Newydd was begun in 1592 on the site of an earlier house by John Panton, Recorder of Denbigh, as one of the most ambitious and sophisticated Elizabethan houses in Wales. Panton was certainly making a big statement to his peers regarding his wealth and success, similar to Sir John Trevor when building Plas Teg near to Mold a few years later during the early 1600s. Cadw states that Plas Teg is the closest parallel to Foxhall Newydd outside of England, as both are products of the Serlian court circle architecture promoted by Smythson, Thorpe and their contemporaries.

Never fully completed but envisaged as a symmetrical H-plan house, what survives today is only one third of what was originally intended. The finished section was, however, inhabited up to the end of the eighteenth century but by the end of the nineteenth it was already ruinous. It is said that due to the lack of partition walls, the oak wainscotting decayed leading to its rapid dereliction.

The Problem

Even for people of imagination and drive this property is a significant challenge; it is without a roof and is also situated in the centre of a large farm. Nevertheless, it is far too important to be left to its own devices to fall down over the next twenty years or so. At the very least, it is a challenge for somebody to consolidate the ruins. This inevitably prompts the question of who is to pay and for what purpose. Nearby, there is the very delightful dovecot which again will be lost if nothing at all happens in terms of consolidation. Maybe that is to be the fate of Foxhall, Newydd, and that part of our common heritage.

Future Thoughts and Possibilities

Yes, this property is indeed of great archaeological and architectural interest, but let us not deceive ourselves into thinking that the next generation will benefit from it if we do nothing in the meantime. In many ways, it has much in common with some Scottish castles in a similar state of dereliction that have, nevertheless, been restored to residential use without unduly compromising its heritage status. In theory, there is no reason why a roof that covered the building until well into the nineteenth century could not be put back on again and the building become a delightful family home or holiday cottage in a setting of truly Arcadian peace and quiet. Perhaps The Landmark or a similar Trust might be interested.

House Listing Grade – I
Gardens Listing Grade – I
Authority – Gwynedd County Council

DESCRIPTION

Glynllifon was the seat of the Glynn family until 1700, when the estate passed by marriage to Thomas Wynn of Boduan. His grandson, Sir Thomas Wynn, became an Irish peer as the first Lord Newborough in 1776. According to the 1873 return of owners of land, Lord Newborough owned an estimated 28,800 acres in Wales (in Caernarfonshire, Merionethshire, Denbighshire and Anglesey), worth an estimated rental of £22,728. This part of the estate remained with the family up until 1948, when it was sold. The house and park were then subsequently sold in 1954 to Caernarvonshire County Council for use as an agricultural college; the estate yard and part of the park first opened to the public in 1989 and is now managed by the Development Directorate of Gwynedd Council. The mansion was sold separately from the park in 2003 for

£500,000; the new owner's plan was to transform the house into a hotel, although there is little evidence of this 'on the ground' at the time of inspection.

There have been at least four houses on the site including the present building. The first Glynllifon was constructed circa 1600 and rebuilt in 1751; this house was described in 1812 as a 'moderate-sized brick mansion having a colonnaded vestibule for its principle entrance' which is now preserved as the kitchen entrance. It was severely damaged by fire in 1836 but was immediately rebuilt in 1836-48 by Edward Haycock of Shrewsbury in the classical style. The house was extended again to the west in 1889-90 with a big kitchen courtyard and service wing.

THE PROBLEM

Had Dr. Zhivago been filmed here one would not be in the least surprised. This great house, home to a great family, was simply too large, and the inheritance too wide for it to have survived in its original use; it had at least two other wonderful houses with not quite so large amounts of accommodation. Certainly it survived the war but was sold shortly thereafter. Although used initially as an agricultural college, it has now been divided from the estate and is in separate ownership. A planning application for conversion to hotel use was made recently, little work appeared to have been done at the time of inspection, and we are told that the poor house may yet again on the market for sale.

FUTURE THOUGHTS AND POSSIBILITIES

Until quite recently this house and its surrounding estate within its enormous stone walls was virtually in one ownership-- and public ownership at that. What a pity, therefore, that no inspired use was identified for this exceptional survivor to benefit the cultural life of Wales to its greatest possible extent. The gardens here are exquisite and have the potential to become again an attraction of international standing. How wonderful it would be if an inspired official could envisage this house becoming the home, say, for the national portrait collection of Wales, or indeed some similar cultural use. The estate yard is already open as a delightful rural museum and there is no reason why the main house could not contribute massively to the appeal of this part of north Wales. It just needs one inspired person with courage and determination to make it happen: if the proposed hotel use actually takes shape, and in a way that does not damage the setting of the house, then we can all heave a sigh of relief.

House Listing Grade – II
Gardens Listing Grade – II*
Authority – Carmarthenshire

DESCRIPTION

Originally, Golden Grove or Gelli Aur was the seat of the Vaughans from circa 1560 to 1804. This family built the Elizabethan mansion which was then subsequently destroyed by fire in 1729. It was rebuilt after many years of dereliction in 1755 - 7 by John Vaughan of Shenfield. This Georgian house was then demolished in 1826 under the instruction of John Frederick Campbell (of Stackpole Court, Pembrokeshire and Cawdor Castle, Nairn, to whom the estate had passed by inheritance) who commissioned the architect Jeffrey Wyattville (then working at Windsor Castle) to design a new house further up the hill, as its original position had been criticised by visitors as being unworthy of a great estate.

This latest house is what remains extant today; it is in Elizabethan style, with crowstepped gables of Llangyndeyrn limestone, and formed a secondary seat for the Earls Cawdor, with a marked similarity to the Duke of Sutherland's house of Lillieshall, Salop by the same architect. Interestingly, the Cawdors were related to the Sutherlands which is perhaps why both houses were designed by Wyattville. In 1952, the house, park and home farm were leased to the County Council for use as an Agricultural Institute. A few years ago it was sold once again, although the park was retained by the Council as a country park.

THE PROBLEM

One cannot resist the temptation to quote Shakespeare: 'blow, blow thou winter wind, thou was never so unkind as man's ingratitude.' How could it be that this great house, which is now at risk, was until relatively recently one of two mansions on that mighty Welsh estate in the ownership of the Earls Cawdor? Sadly, the Welsh estate is no more, having been sold up almost entirely during the latter part of the last century. This has been something of a cultural catastrophe for Wales with the demolition of Stackpole Court and the dispersal of its contents. Golden Grove was the family's Carmathenshire seat and is spectacularly sited on rising ground in the vale of Towy. After many years' use as an agricultural college, it was sold off and has been a real problem ever since.

FUTURE THOUGHTS AND POSSIBILITIES

Strangely enough, this is not a vast house and the immediate pleasure gardens are quite constrained. It is therefore quite feasible for it to become a private family house again, given sufficient will and determination of all those concerned. This requires an enlightened approach by the Local Authority and the owner of the mansion. Between the two, surely there is a wonderful opportunity to create a truly saleable holding that could once again play its full part in the life of South Wales and the Towy Valley, either as a private home or hotel or as a private home with holiday cottages in the stables.

THE GRANGE HOTEL, RHYL

House Listing Grade – II
Authority – Denbighshire County Council

DESCRIPTION

Pleasantly situated prominently on the promenade, Snowdonia can be seen in the distance above the sweep of the North Wales coast. Built during the 1840s as two separate villas called Morannedd and Boddonnan, the houses were prime in their day and highly sought-after residences. During the mid 1890s, for instance, Michael Antonio Ralli was residing at Morannedd and was nominated as Sherriff for Flintshire in 1896 and 1897. A lithograph from the mid 1850s shows how prominent the pair of villas were in relation to the architectural setting of this section of Rhyl. They were subsequently joined up and developed as a hotel.

On Tuesday, 18th March 2008, the fire brigade was called out to fight a blaze in the western portion of the building; a fire apparently accidentally started by squatters who had lit candles. A chimney and part of the rear section of the west wing were demolished as unsafe, yet this has had a minimal effect on how the building is viewed from the promenade. The Local Authority has stated that demolition is a serious consideration despite strong opposition from the Victorian Society and local residents. Immediate action is urgently required to safeguard the building from further destruction.

The Problem

These two houses are certainly big architectural statements on the seafront at Rhyl and in some ways are a little out of place as a result– a busy seafront is not the best of settings for high quality residential property, although of course this use ceased many years ago. Up to December 2006, the two houses were in use as a hotel in an area that is not overburdened with fine architecture. Thus there may be an incentive to ensure that the whole site is redeveloped, rather than make every effort to conserve and build on what is there.

Future Thoughts and Possibilities

We suspect that there may be little will for these good buildings to be secured in the long term. This would be a pity as they certainly smack of quality and can assert a beneficial influence over a wide part of the surrounding area. Thus there is no reason why the fire could not prompt the creation of a fine hotel within the existing structures or indeed a concession to residential flats. Let us hope that the local planning authority will be able to demonstrate that they are exerting every effort to ensure these buildings are given a long term future for the benefit of transient holiday makers, as well as for the nation.

House Listing Grade – II
Authority – Vale of Glamorgan

DESCRIPTION

It was at Great Frampton, austere, elegant yet with a dignity prevalent among many Welsh gentry and their houses, that the renowned astronomer Nathaniel Pigott resided during the late 1770s. Pigott erected an observatory in the grounds and his astronomical observations from Frampton were published by the Royal Society; he famously discovered a 'nebula' in Coma Berenices, recorded on 23rd March 1779 at the house. Great Frampton is of sixteenth century origin with extensive alterations in the seventeenth century and a fashionable façade was built during the mid-eighteenth century complete with stone balls on the parapet. For many years, Great Frampton was in the hands of the Wilkins family, who leased the estate out to tenant farmers; one in particular, Lloyd Williams, was declared bankrupt in 1885 but died shortly before the order was served. The Board family are then associated with the two-hundred and fifty acre estate; they continued its use as a farm. Old Mr Board had been a gardener in Devon and walked all the way to Wales with only 1s in his pocket to begin a new life. He became a bailiff to the owner of Great Frampton, and showing great aptitude as well as initiative, was eventually able to take over the estate. During the 1930s, his son was famed for his herd of cross-bred Aberdeen Angus and Dairy Shorthorn cows, winning many awards for Frampton.

Today, the building is a dramatic yet forlorn shell, despite having been refurbished in the

1970s. It was put up for sale in 1990 and was on the market for at least two years. Tragically, it was completely gutted by fire in December 1994, yet the rear wing escaped the blaze. But it is now derelict due to vandalism and neglect. One of the most remarkable survivals which has now been revealed is a projecting sixteenth century stair turret which is in astonishingly good condition. The Vale of Glamorgan County Council have identified that, despite being damaged by fire, the structure remains sound enough to consider rescue to be justifiable in listed building terms. An Urgent Works Notice and Repair Notice have both been considered to safeguard the surviving buildings at this delightful Georgian

THE PROBLEM

The problem here is perhaps no more than an illustration of how enigmatic the human race can be. Here we have the most delightful small manor house, ideally situated in the Vale of Glamorgan, close to Cardiff, which should have potential rescuers queuing up from the site to the sea. Yet what we have in reality is a burnt out shell with a degree of uncertainty as to its ownership, yet it is a major component of our built heritage. Perhaps it is no more than an unfortunate combination of circumstances that allows this building to continue as a wreck all of fourteen years since the fire.

FUTURE THOUGHTS AND POSSIBILITIES

Surely there must be someone in Cardiff, Bridgend or Port Talbot who wants a family home of distinction in the Vale of Glamorgan. It may only be a question of searching out the relevant people for the main part of the problem to be solved. Indeed, the current owner may overcome whatever problems that he or she may have, and wish to rescue this delightful building as a family home for themselves. Although much of the historic fabric has been lost, this does mean that whoever rescues the building will have much freedom to incorporate their own design ideas for the benefit of posterity this time around, which may in time be regarded as heritage items sometime in the future. What does the crystal ball have in store for this property over the next ten years? Watch this space to find out.

Gwrych Castle, Abergele

A Case Study

House Listing Grade – I
Gardens Listing Grade – II*
Authority – Conwy County Borough Council

Description

Magnificently perched above the Bay of Liverpool, Gwrych Castle is surrounded by superabundant greenery. Work on site was commissioned in 1819 on the orders of Lloyd Hesketh Bamford-Hesketh, with Thomas Rickman acting as architect and general advisor. The nucleus of the main house was finished by 1822, but Bamford-Hesketh continued extending the house up until 1854. His son Robert employed George Edmund Street to design a private chapel and possibly the great Italian marble staircase as well in 1870. Robert's daughter, the Countess of Dundonald by marriage, extended the house further with bedroom accommodation between 1909 - 1914.

Following her death in 1924, the estate was bought back by her husband from the Church in Wales (who had inherited it) but the house remained uninhabited until it was eventually sold off in 1946. From 1948 to 1985 the castle successfully functioned as a major tourist attraction and cultural centre, until lack of adequate repair caused it to be closed. It was subsequently sold to a California property developer who allowed the building to be stripped, vandalised and taken over by New Age Travellers. It was only after pressure from the Gwrych Castle Building Preservation Trust that the building was recently put up for sale following nearly twenty years of abandonment. In this time the entire property had become ruinous and roofless but still exceptionally picturesque; it then attracted a UK-based property development company who purchased it privately from the American for restoration and conversion into a hotel. Preliminary work started in early 2008.

As one of Wales' most important castellated mansions, Gwrych is also one of Europe's earliest in the nineteenth century. With interiors by C.A. Busby and Crace, it became one of the most sumptuous country houses along the North Wales coast. Based primarily on the Edwardian castles of Conwy, Rhuddlan and Beaumaris, it is one of the most successful replications of medieval architecture. The gardens at Gwrych are based around an ancient yew tree woodland which has stands nearly five hundred years old. Evidence survives of the previous house which was Elizabethan in origin and the drives leading to it which may have also been part of the old highway. Various folly towers, garden temples, obelisks, ornamental bridges as well as conservatories and terraces survive from the early part of the nineteenth century, forming an important collection of Regency garden architecture. The main staircase is one of the longest anywhere.

The Problem

One truly must pinch oneself to be certain that this diabolical mess was actually allowed to happen. To think that a house of this importance and this quality which was earning its way as a major tourist attraction so recently could be bought for ready cash and then abandoned strains one's credibility. But this is what actually happened; as a result Gwrych is, at the time of writing, little more than a vandalised shell, a major part of which has already collapsed. We are therefore witnessing the agonies of an astonishing cultural asset. So, in terms of scale alone, the rescue of this building is going to be a significant challenge for the new owners who, nevertheless, appear to have the determination, resilience and strength of will to overcome all problems with this very large building. What a pity that so much of the historic fabric has been lost; that can never be returned. For all too long it has been a matter of 'his castle – our heritage' and the gap between the two was nothing less than a gulch!

Future Thoughts and Possibilities

What a relief and delight it is to be able to do no more than to wish these remarkable new owners the best of good fortune in rescuing this noble building for the benefit of our heritage, tourism and the good people of Abergele. Indeed, the projected use of the building as a hotel seems to be closest in keeping with the private house which it always was, although this time around the guests will be paying whereas hitherto they did not! It is still very early days, but the signs are most encouraging in that no significant enabling development seems to be on the cards.

Gwylfa Hiraethog, Bryn Trillyn, Denbigh Moors

House Listing Grade – Unlisted
Authority – Denbighshire County Council

Description

High on the barren moor land, atop a peak called Bryn Trillyn, was built a shooting lodge and summer residence for Hudson Ewbanke Kearley, later the first Lord Devonport. The original house was christened Plas Pren, as it was a wooden Norwegian chalet imported in 1898 and erected on site. It leaked tremendously and the whole building later became encased in stone when it became one of the grandest Edwardian retreats in Britain. Edward VII is said to have been entertained here and Lloyd George presented a speech from one of its balconies. Lord Devonport decided to sell the estate in 1925 preferring to spend his time on his Scottish estates. Gwylfa Hiraethog was then purchased by a consortium who continued to use it as a shoot right up until the outbreak of World War 2, at which point the building began gently to decline.

Although a caretaker lived in the house until it was sold by its then owner, a Manchester brewery, to local lady, Dora Roberts. Mrs. Roberts owned Gwylfa for nearly 30 years, but in this time the house fell into severe decay. The elaborate plasterwork and panelling all rotted, the strong wind blew off slates, and thieves stole the lead, yet nothing was done to rectify the situation. A final ray of hope appeared in 1983 when the estate was put up for sale again, still within easy reach of restoration. Alas, this was not to be. Anything of value was removed from the ruins so that collapse was swift, and by the late 1990s Lord Devonport's shooting box was no more than a disfigured stump on the Denbigh Moors. As a further insult to the pitiful ruins, the placement of a mobile phone mast on site obliterated parts of its service section. It is now little more than a pile of stones.

The Problem

Oh dear, what a problem we have here. As the photograph rightly shows, there is very little of this building left. However, it has been included because it demonstrates so well how quickly a problem building can become little more than a pile of stones; in less than twenty years in this instance. In some ways, perhaps, this has always been a problem building in that it is sited high up on the Denbigh moors in a position that could not be more exposed; there is not even a single tree growing within half a mile. 'Bleak house' could have been a most apt alternative description.

Future Thoughts and Possibilities

When looking at these ruins one's thoughts are bound to veer again toward Scotland and its proliferation of fine shooting lodges which continue as a joy to behold. However, we wanted to include this because it illustrates so well how buildings are lost over relatively short periods of time if the roof is taken off and the walls remain unconsolidated. We are told that, just forty years ago, this building was inhabited by a gamekeeper, and indeed many can remember it roofed over not much more than twenty years ago. And yet here it is, little more than a pile of stones gradually being subsumed into the moors of Denbigh. Consolidation and urgent recording could be considered, if it is not already too late.

House Listing Grade – II
Park & Gardens Listing Grade – NOT LISTED
Authority – Gwynedd County Council

DESCRIPTION

In the south-east corner of the Lleyn Peninsula, overlooking Cardigan Bay to the south and lifting the eye to a grand panorama of the Snowdonian mountain range to the east, lies Gwynfryn, resplendent in a refined parkland where ancient oaks and the remnants of Victorian ornamental planting still endure. Associated with the esteemed Wynne family, the estate passed by marriage to David Ellis of Bodychan during the mid-seventeenth century. His great-great grandson, also named David Ellis, added the surname Nanney on inheriting Cefndeuddwr from his bachelor uncle; he became attorney general for North Wales under the Great Sessions dispensation. No lawyer in North Wales was said to have been held in higher esteem than David during the early nineteenth century, and his knowledge combined

of common law and good common sense was renowned. He died without issue in 1819 and left the estate to his nephew, Owen Jones of Brynhir, who assumed the additional surnames of Ellis-Nanney as a condition of his inheritance.

Owen Jones Ellis-Nanney was described as a 'bucolic character, and a thorough-going Welshman, indistinguishable at sight from the neighbouring farmers; indeed he would

at times take a delight in being mistaken for an out-of-work farmhand, and would ask a stranger, met when out for a walk, if there was any chance of getting a job at the Plas.' Owen's young wife died four years after giving birth to a son and heir, Hugh John Ellis-Nanney, in 1849. Owen purchased the neighbouring Plas Hen estate, adding hugely to his lands, which was settled on his young son and heir. Hugh was educated at Eton and Oxford, becoming a firm Conservative and a most eligible bachelor.

On his twenty-first birthday, Hugh came of age and set about elevating the standing of his family home. George Williams was employed as architect, building a baronial mansion in the castellated style, similar to nearby Deudraeth Castle. The house was approached by a grand, full size porte-cochere opening onto a top-lit central stair hall. The dining room suite lay to the service side of the castle, and the parlour and other reception rooms to the front. Work was completed in 1876 and estimated to have cost nearly £70,000 – a prodigiously large expenditure in those far off days.

Hugh married the Hon. Elizabeth Octavia Dillon, younger daughter of the third Lord Clonbrock. The marriage produced two children, the eldest, Mary Elizabeth eventually inherited the estate while a son died tragically at the age of eight whilst on holiday at Bournemouth, much to the grief of his parents. Hugh was deeply interested in politics, becoming M.P. for Caernarfonshire and one of the strongest candidates brought forward against Lloyd George in 1895, being defeated by only 194 votes. In 1897, Hugh was created a baronet and enjoyed the last twenty-three years of his life happily at Gwynfryn. Lady Elizabeth followed him a few years later

in 1928. Daughter Mary Elizabeth moved from Gwynfryn to Plas Hen, renaming it Plas Talhenbont and leased the Gwynfryn mansion to the Church in Wales as a home for the clergy. It was sold off when the estate was broken up in 1959, becoming first a hospital for the elderly and then a hotel. During the early 1980s, while under redevelopment, the house mysteriously caught fire and was gutted. A squatter took over in more recent times, attempting to carry out repairs but was evicted before trying to claim the building as his own. Presently, there are no plans in place for its future as the owner is believed to be abroad.

THE PROBLEM

Clearly this noble pile of building is burnt out; that's problem number one. Number two is that there is evidence of structural weakness to the tower that needs fairly urgent attention if a costly collapse is to be prevented. Number three is that the house will fall down if nothing is done to consolidate the walls which are open to the elements.

FUTURE THOUGHTS AND POSSIBILITIES

Well you lucky punters out there, here again is another opportunity to consider a great house in a delightful position with exquisite views towards Harlech and beyond. The approach is like a voyage of discovery down a wooded drive opening out into a sheltered park as gradually the mansion reveals itself as one proceeds; it is all redolent of the Alec Guinness film 'Kind Hearts and Coronets.' It could certainly make a hotel, but probably a fine family home would be nearer the mark. It is not so large and could provide some eight suites of bedroom, bathroom and dressing room, but probably no more. If an owner can pull this off, he or she will have a family home of huge presence.

HAY CASTLE

House Listing Grade – I
Gardens Listing Grade – II
Authority – Powys County Council

DESCRIPTION

Situated on the south side of Hay-on-Wye, the castle stands high above this town of books. Originally built between 1200 and 1211 by Marcher Lord William de Braose and his wife Matilda, it was reconstructed by Henry III in 1233 following the sacking of the town by Llewelyn ap Gruffudd. After further attacks during the fifteenth century, the castle became part of the mighty Beaufort Estates. Howell Gwynne erected a Jacobean house alongside the keep between 1600 and 1650 which was then replaced by another built for James Boyle in 1660.

The castle was let from the Wellington family to Joseph Bailey who purchased the manor in 1844. It was then mostly leased to the local clergy with the old keep being used as a lock-up for the town. In 1906, the castle became the home of the first Dowager Lady Glanusk and then, in about 1910, the house was partly restored by the architect Caroe. The Baileys eventually decided to sell it off in 1937. Fire ravaged the eastern half of the property soon after in 1939; in 1977 the western portion was badly damaged by fire but has since been restored. Sadly, the eastern half remains a shell.

The Problem

It is a pity that this building is officially considered to be at risk, primarily, we imagine, on account of the large areas that are no more than a shell following destruction by fire. The worry here is that the unroofed areas will simply deteriorate further over the years to the point of instability if the roof is not replaced.

Future Thoughts and Possibilities

Again, we are not alone to consider this to be one of the great medieval houses of Wales, dominating this fine border village with its annual literary festival. Anyone could consider themselves blessed to own such an asset, but how much more blessed an owner could be by roofing over the vulnerable parts of the building to guarantee, as much as anyone can, the survival of the building in its present form. Doing all that is necessary to keep options open for future generations would appear to be the most worthwhile of challenges for the immediate future, this may involve consolidation of the unroofed sections of the building. We wish those responsible the best of good fortune

House Listing Grade – I
Gardens Listing Grade – II
Authority – Conwy County Borough Council

DESCRIPTION

Situated close by the village of Llangernyw, Hafodunos Hall was designed by Sir Gilbert Scott (designer of St Pancras Station) between 1861 and 1866 for Henry Robertson Sandbach, whose family had bought the estate in 1830. The new house replaced one which had been built in 1674, although the site had been occupied since at least 1530. Scott was amongst the most

house in high regard, emphasing its importance as the finest Victorian Gothic house in Wales.

The style is Venetian-inspired Gothic, predominantly of two storeys with an attic, built in soft red brick with diaper work and extensive stone dressings to windows and doors. The garden front is by far the most impressive

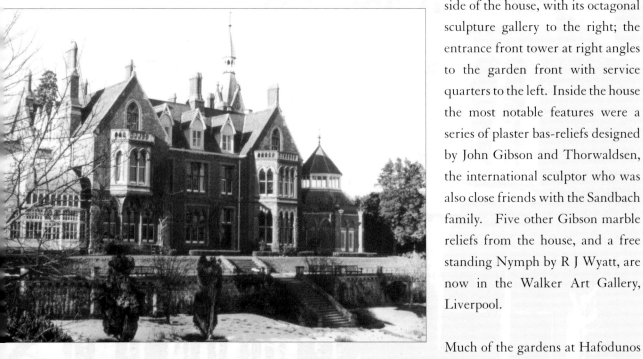

side of the house, with its octagonal sculpture gallery to the right; the entrance front tower at right angles to the garden front with service quarters to the left. Inside the house the most notable features were a series of plaster bas-reliefs designed by John Gibson and Thorwaldsen, the international sculptor who was also close friends with the Sandbach family. Five other Gibson marble reliefs from the house, and a free standing Nymph by R J Wyatt, are now in the Walker Art Gallery, Liverpool.

widely acclaimed Gothic Revival architects and thus a proponent of the Gothic style in domestic architecture. Hafodunos is considered second only to Kelham Hall, Nottinghamshire, in Gilbert Scott's domestic output, and the only example of his country house style in Wales. His son, John Oldrid Scott, was later employed in 1883 to design the elaborate conservatories built by Messenger. Sir John Betjamin held the

Much of the gardens at Hafodunos date from the mid to late nineteenth century, except for the late seventeenth – early eighteenth century walled garden. The Sandbach family had been advised by Hooker of Kew on the planting of the gardens, which are laid out in terraces and along a small valley which meanders in front of the house. Today, the gardens are overgrown, but eminently capable of straight forward restoration, and still very enticing.

The Problem

Hafodunos shut down as an old people's home in 1993 and no suitable alternative long term use was discovered thereafter. Dry rot became a problem, spreading through the servants' quarters into the main house. By 1998, Conwy Council were contemplating serving an Urgent Works Notice on the then owner but his unfortunate death left the estate in the hands of executors. Hafodunos was then put on the commercial market for sale again and was eventually bought in 2001 by a local developer for less than £300,000. During the late spring of 2004, he unveiled plans for a hotel, one hundred plus log cabins and Caravan Park, but on the night of 13th October the house was the victim of a devastating fire– arson– which gutted the main block. However, the conservatories and service wing remained virtually untouched, even though they were much in need of repair. Efforts to board up the site failed to prevent further vandalism including the removal of Gibson bas-reliefs. The building was yet again put on the commercial market in 2006 for £800,000 but failed to sell. As of April 2008, the house and gardens has been placed officially on the market by receivers.

Future Thoughts and Possibilities

This is arguably one of the worst losses of architectural heritage of Wales for a generation, and probably should be regarded as a 'wake up call' concerning Welsh heritage. How sad that immediately before the fire its future was being fought over like a bone amongst a pack of wolves, yet in retrospect the two most important issues of all, security and maintenance, had been ignored for years. Nevertheless, whilst the shell seems sound enough to justify a measure of restoration, the planners and amenity societies must avoid the temptation of asking for too much lofty restoration of potential rescuers. Pragmatism should be the order of the day. Let us hope that the property will be put fully on the market at a sufficiently realistic price as to attract that single hero out there whose love of the Venetian Gothic will save what is left for themselves, and posterity. The site alone is 'to die for.' We should expect responsible marketing by the current vendors who must avoid just dumping the property on some hopeful dreamer without funds to rescue this sumputous home. We have seen just this happen time and time again, it should not be repeated.

ST JOHN THE BAPTIST, SLEBECH

Church Listing Grade – II
Authority – Pembrokeshire County Council

DESCRIPTION

This impressive yet austerely imposing church has stood empty since its 1990 closure supposedly due to subsidence. It was built 1838 – 40 by J.H. Good Junior for Baron de Rutzen of nearby Slebech Hall as a replacement for the medieval church deemed too close to the hall itself. Slebech Church was intended to serve the neighbouring parishes of Minwear and Newton North and was built with contributions to the construction costs from Queen Adelaide and the Duchess of Kent. It was not until 1848 that the new church was consecrated following various disputes regarding the redundant church near the Hall.

Unusually orientated to the north-east, it is claimed that this was due to the problem of finding dry ground for setting the foundations. Most of the interior, such as the painted scheme of 1893 by C. E. G. Gray of Cambridge, has either been removed or is badly damaged. Today, this lonely church stands without much protection from vandals who have already broken into the crypt beneath the nave; the rest of the structure could well be at risk if action is not taken soon.

The Problem

The problem here would appear to be that this wonderful, prominent Pembrokeshire landmark almost at the entrance to Haverfordwest (the county town) has for so long been unloved. It really is spectacularly sited and, with its exotic mid-Victorian silhouette, it dominates the surrounding area. Let us not forget that, once lost, we're most unlikely, ever to see such a property being built again this side of heaven.

Future Thoughts and Possibilities

Given the building's prominence and quality it is submitted that this is a building that should not be lost whatever the cost of keeping it up. It is, therefore, up to the people of Pembrokeshire and all relevant authorities to seek out and finance a viable new use for this venerable building. The county would not be the same without it.

Listing Grade – II*
Authority – Cardiff City Council

DESCRIPTION

Built first in 1855 as Ely Court by W. G. & E. Habershon for James Harvey Insole, a colliery and shipping owner, it was extended in 1873 by G. E. Robinson, then greatly enlarged again in 1875 by James, Seward and Thomas, architects of Cardiff, which included fine internal remodelling influenced by work at Cardiff Castle by the Pugin inspired Gothicist William Burges. The house was once again extended by Seward in 1898 and later by William Clarke and Sons, the renowned Llandaff masons who had contributed much of the earlier building work. Completed in 1906-9, the house became known as 'The Court.' The estate was sold separately from the house to Cardiff City Corporation in 1932 when the land adjoining was developed, metamorphosing into Western Avenue and much of the surrounding housing. The Insole family left the house itself in 1938 and, despite a horrific fire in 1939, it became the Cardiff Headquarters of the Air Raid Precautions during World War Two, now under the name of Insole Court.

Since the war, with yet another name change to Llandaff Court, it has had various community uses including a public library which remained there until the late 1970s. It then fell into disuse and decay and was threatened with demolition until, after much public protest, it was repaired and conserved in 1995 back to much of its 1909 appearance. Since then, it has been a conference and other community uses centre, once again under the name of Insole Court. The building was closed by the Local Authority in November 2006 due to presence of asbestos; it is rumoured that it will reopen in the autumn of 2008.

THE PROBLEM

There is an air of unreality about Insole Court; it is situated in a residential area between Llandaff and Cardiff, forming a little oasis of architectural splendour. Yet there seems to be no secure use envisaged; the stables are in severe disrepair and generally the property, especially its buildings, are crying out for a little TLC. Paradoxically though, the gardens appear to be well-kept and thus a joy for the local residents despite some bouts of petty vandalism. The property is in public ownership at present.

FUTURE THOUGHTS AND POSSIBILITIES

Whether in public or private ownership, this house and garden are intrinsically magnificent. How lucky the residents of Cardiff are to have this in their midst! Bearing in mind that it was built as a private house and that its architectural coherence is best safe-guarded by a use that respects this aspect, it should not be too difficult for the city council to come up with a public use that really does make the most of every facet of this jewel. Yes, the running costs will always be high, but the cultural returns should be commensurate. We wish the best of good fortune to the decision-makers in whose hands the future of this building rests; previous generations here could not have done more to endow their successors on an almost princely scale – this is the real meaning of heritage.

Iscoed, Ferryside

Listing Grade – II
Authority – Carmarthenshire County Council

Description

Iscoed was begun in April 1772 for Sir William Mansel, possibly with Anthony Keck as the architect. Constructed in red brick (unusual for this part of Wales) with pavilion wings, Iscoed is magnificently situated overlooking Carmarthen Bay, surrounded by rolling, unspoilt countryside. The mansion was sold to Wellington's colleague Sir Thomas Picton in 1812, who carried out further works and indeed it remained in the family until 1919. It was then purchased by a certain Glendinning Moxham of Swansea who repaired it and carried out minor alterations including the addition of a conservatory. After World War Two, Iscoed became council owned flats and was subsequently stripped of its internal fittings and roof.

In 1957 its listing as a building of historic importance was refused, enabling permission to be granted for demolition which thankfully was never implemented due to the applicant's sudden death. It was sold during the early 1980s when one wing was re-roofed but the Local Authority astonishingly refused permission to restore the main block. An appeal to the Welsh Office was successful and some work took place in 1982. The ruined stable block located not very far from the main house seems to be in separate ownership, but it is sufficiently distant so as not to harm Iscoed's amenity. It has been remarked that Iscoed is perhaps in better condition than Piercefield, St. Arvans, which has been placed on the market with full plans for restoration. This should give much hope for the dejected ruins of Iscoed!

The Problem

For some, the problem is that this exceptional and exquisite house occupies one of the most sublime sites in Wales with long views down the Towy estuary and onto the sea; it is all so beautiful 'that it hurts.' Maybe such over-enthusiasm is synonymous with the rose-tinted glasses one inevitably needs when tackling great challenges. Iscoed does undoubtedly represent a challenge; although consisting only of four rooms per floor in the main house, the service accommodation is large comprising of two flanking wings on either side of the house which are connected by parallel range to the rear. Some of these rooms have been substantially rescued but the remainder is roofless. No doubt the house itself has some structural defects but none that appear to be in any way terminal.

Future Thoughts and Possibilities

For the last sixty years or so this house has been typical of its type, in that it is eminently suitable for rescue. The solutions are almost endless in that the house itself is not huge so that even a modest rescue operation could be limited to reinstating the roof and perhaps the ground and first floor only. This would still provide one with an exquisite house in one of the finest sites in the UK. Any further rescue operation, perhaps including provision for holiday accommodation, would then be a bonus once the future of the main house had been secured. Indeed, for some it is quite possible that the house could not provide adequate space, so further accommodation in one of the flanking wings would be an ideal solution. There is, therefore, no reason why this wonderful property should be lost. Indeed, what a shame it is that, in an area so near to Cardiff, Swansea, Llanelli and Neath, this great Welsh mansion went into the 21st century roofless. It is perhaps an indictment of us all, but in all likelihood this problem house will be freely rescued 'ere long. It certainly deserves to be, and is rumoured to be on the market at the time of writing.

Kinmel Park Listing Grade – I
Stable Block – II*
Gardens Listing Grade – II*
Authority – Conwy County Borough Council

DESCRIPTION

Present-day Kinmel is the third incarnation of a house on this site. It is enormous. The old hall, which is now in the walled garden, dates back to the seventeenth century and is entirely ruinous; it comprises only a few walls remain standing amidst a jungle of overgrowth. Since the departure of the Hughes family during the summer of 1929 to nearby Kinmel Manor, the Nesfield mansion has had a sad and chequered history. Kinmel School opened on September 24th 1929, but closed due to financial difficulties in 1934. In 1936, a Rheuma Spa was opened, not too dissimilar to the exclusive health spas of today; it was breaking even, maybe even making a small profit when abruptly the house

was requisitioned by the army and the Spa was given twelve days to vacate. During the war, Kinmel was used as a military hospital up until the Autumn of 1945 when the keys were handed back to the owners of the Rheuma Spa. During 1946 it reopened as a Hotel and Osteopathic Clinic but was shut down in 1948 following the illegal sale of alcohol on the premises. A private girl's school from Malvern, Clarendon School, closely followed and continued successfully for some twenty-seven years.

In 1975 the house was harmed by a savage fire, but this was mainly restricted to the roof and service areas, so the main rooms survived relatively untouched. The house and grounds reverted back to the original family who sought out various possibilities, including demolition of the damaged buildings. However, a local businessman eventually emerged who offered to reinstate the house and turn it into a Christian conference centre; a 999 year lease was prepared with the first ninety-nine years at peppercorn rent on the proviso the facades were restored. Work was spread out over several years with the aid of generous Welsh Office grants and bank loans, thus enabling various parts of the house to open for the use intended.

The Problem

One would not be too surprised to find this huge building, with its grounds and stables of distinction, on the banks of the Loire, open to the public as the pride of the French nation! There is no reason why similar circumstances should not prevail with this building on the North Wales coast, near Abergele. It is large by anyone's standard and, whilst it did suffer a serious fire some years ago, the damage appears to have been adequately repaired, even though

further roof works may be required. Thus, on account of its size, it would seem unlikely that this would revert for use as a private house. The problem, in essence, is that the structure is little more than a fantastic huge house with no apparent use. We believe that there is an urgent need to rectify a serious outbreak of dry rot in the house.

Future Thoughts and Possibilities

This property is grade I and is truly outstanding, yet it has been 'bouncing along on its bottom' for far too long, including appearances in auctions in the commercial property market. It is hugely important as a cultural asset and so deserves better than this. At present, it appears to be in limbo, just waiting for rescue by a lively entrepreneur who can turn the challenges of its great size into tangible assets, whether as a hotel, conference centre, residential flats or some other use. But, in any event, it is absolutely vital that the building continues to be properly and adequately maintained so that all options are kept open. What an exceptional opportunity for the right person!

Llantwit Place or Old Place, Llantwit Major

Scheduled Ancient Monument
House Listing Grade – II
Authority – Vale of Glamorgan County Council

Description

Leland wrote in the 1530s that Llantwit Place was the residence of Edmund Van, a descendent of the Vans of Marcross. It seems to be the case that the mansion was home to the eldest sons of the family; towards the end of the sixteenth century the grandson of Edmund Van enlarged the house at the expense of his father-in-law, Griffith William. In about 1694, the estate was left jointly to heiresses and thus inevitably was sold out of the family. Its subsequent history is unknown, but by the middle of the nineteenth century it was recorded as being in very poor condition. The house is made up of three building phases; the early house incorporated into the rear wing, the main central range with hall and parlour, then two wings containing the kitchen and another parlour, whilst at the same time a pillar stair was constructed at the rear of the house. Additionally, during the early seventeenth century the gardens were developed and a pair of forecourts constructed.

Llantwit Place is today under the ownership of Glamorgan Council who, in 2006, tried to sell it at auction at a guide price of £5000 - £15,000. Cadw stated that as a Scheduled Ancient Monument the Council was required to consult them regarding its future before any sale could take place; consequently the building was removed from sale.

The Problem

It does not take too much of a stretch of the imagination to visualise this house in Elizabethan times– it is quite grand and enough of it remains for a rescue operation to be worthwhile. What a shame that it is now roofless and parts of the walls appear in distress. It sits in a raised position, with excellent views over the village of Llantwit Major. However, if something is not done, at least a consolidation of the ruins, then this, like so many other buildings, could be lost quite needlessly. Yes, it is a romantic ruin, but it is simply unrealistic to think that a private individual is going to care for it as a romantic ruin indefinitely.

Future Thoughts and Possibilities

With time, care, a sensitive, delicate hand, this building could be re-roofed and put back in use as a house, maybe even open to the public.

What a great opportunity to reinstate missing elements in a sensitive and scholarly way! This is a typical example of an opportunity to create today the heritage of tomorrow, whilst at the same time protecting the heritage of the past. It is most encouraging, therefore, that the property has recently been put up for sale; at least there is no dog in the manger here which can so easily happen with houses like this! Nevertheless, one hopes that the conservation lobby will not be tempted to overbid with excessive requirements from a new owner which could simply result in the building being lost in the long term. This is perhaps an ideal instance where we can take a leaf out of our Scottish neighbour's book: they have encouraged many castles to be re-roofed when in even worse condition than this, the results are usually as moving as they are rewarding.

Llwyn Ynn

House and Stables Listing Grade – II
Authority – Denbighshire County Council

Description

The Parrys reputably built the manor house of Llwyn Ynn during the early sixteenth century and owned it right up until the early twentieth century. Major alterations seem to have taken place in 1672 which are recorded on a date stone under the coat of arms over the main doorway. Apparently, this refers to the period when the house underwent repairs, and a portion of it was pulled down upon ceasing to be the principal residence of its owners. The interiors were said to have been particularly fine and included many old low ceiling halls lined with panelling, the staircase was itself noted as being a 'really fine old oak carved staircase.'

The estate of 2000 acres was broken up in 1912 following its sale for £50,000, chiefly being sold to the tenants. At the close of the auction, during which every purchase by a tenant had been heartily cheered, a vote of thanks was passed to the auctioneer and the vendor's agent for their consideration towards the tenantry. The core area of Llwyn Ynn continued to be a private home until 1937 when the contents of the house, which included many valuable antiques, were sold. Llwyn Ynn hall was demolished during the 1950s, and all that now remains is an east wing which may have been the original medieval hall that was later converted to a service wing for the main house. This is rapidly deteriorating and it is a pity to witness the last vestiges of such a great house just crumbling away.

THE PROBLEM

When entering the park, the visitor really is transported into a Bucolic Idyll well worthy of one of the great French eighteenth century paintings that prompted the picturesque movement; indeed it encourages one to daydream of past glories even though the most recent house has gone. It truly is one of the most delightful parks the authors have visited. But the old house which eventually became the service wing is, glory be, still there. Wonderfully sited beside a rushing stream, the whole place resonates with the past grandeur which could, with adequate imagination, ingenuity and funding be reinstated. Yes, indeed, what is left is semi-derelict but not beyond a challenge and realistic solution, because the setting is so utterly lovely.

FUTURE THOUGHTS AND POSSIBILITIES

Provided that what remains does not proceed into oblivion, there are all the makings of a very fine private home here in the Vale of Clwyd, in an area that has long been recognised as one of the most delectable residential areas in the North West. Planning authorities should therefore approach any rescue operation with significant flexibility so that Llwyn Ynn can once again become on of North Wales' more significant private homes– all the potential is there for current and future owners, not only to resurrect past glories, but to exceed them!

Llethr

House and Stables Listing Grade – II
Authority – Pembrokeshire County Council

Description

The late historian Major Francis Jones states that the earliest reference to Llethr comes from 1328, when John ap Philip granted to 'Adam the clerk' half of a building and garden. For nearly three hundred years the Jones and Roch families owned the manor until, during 1919, it was put up for sale by Colonel Thomas James Roch who was moving to Tenby. The sale catalogue states that the manor house consisted on the ground floor of an entrance hall, dining room, kitchen, scullery, pantry, larder, and boot room. On the first floor was the drawing room, four bedrooms and a dressing room, whilst the second floor had three further bedrooms, a bathroom and W.C. In the grounds were a large lawn tennis court and a walled garden which gave access via an archway onto the first floor of the house.

Llethr is a good example of a Pembrokeshire gentry-house built during the late eighteenth or early nineteenth century, though it may well date from even earlier as the rear wing contains an early eighteenth century staircase. The stucco on the walls is particularly interesting: as it degrades it is revealing the colours of the house over the past two hundred years. Despite its semi-dereliction the house is still occupied, but little maintenance appears to have been carried out for ages and it may not be before long before the house becomes ruinous. Adjacent to Llethr is the elegant vernacular long-lofted stable which is of late eighteenth century date; the nogged brickwork pediment is a particularly charming feature. Two bays were added to the left-hand side of the stable in 1851, possibly to house carts or carriages; generally it is a fine thing of considerable size.

The Problem

It seems to us that the essential problem here is little more than one of funding, aspiration and repair. Essentially, the house is plain but quite grand in terms of scale, especially with a first floor drawing room. But, it is the stables here that have the potential to be a tour-de-force. Sadly, this too is at risk on account of disrepair.

Future Thoughts and Possibilities

It would be a great shame if these two buildings were, in the long run, to be lost simply on account of disrepair, which seems quite possible at the present time. On the other hand, a relatively small amount of funding by way of emergency repairs could keep options open for at least another generation. There is no reason, then, why this delightful ensemble could not again form a family home of much distinction, with any number of possible beneficial uses for the stables. We wish the owners well in facing up to the challenges before them in maintaining their part of the heritage of Wales, and hope that they may receive help in so doing from the various heritage authorities; the buildings certainly deserve all the help it can get.

House Listing Grade – II
Authority – Monmouthshire County Council

DESCRIPTION

An utterly amazing property that has defied the ravages of time and modernisation, this could well be one of the most complete medieval farmhouses to have survived in Wales. Originally an early seventeenth century double unit farmhouse, it was enlarged towards the end of the century at the uphill end. During the nineteenth century very few changes, including refenestration, took place so the house was never Victorianised.

Completely untouched since 1947, the farmhouse was made wind and water tight whilst remaining uninhabited. Some modern farm sheds have been built nearly without compromising the whole, which functioned as a farm up until recently. It has, we believe, in 2006/2007 been purchased by a local businessman. One enters into the stone flagged hall of the early seventeenth century house which still retains its original beamed ceiling; adjoining it is the dairy with original windows still fitted with iron stanchion and an inner shutter. In the late seventeenth century end of the house is the parlour which has a complex renaissance moulding to the ceiling beams.

The Problem

One is not quite sure what the problem is here. Is it that the property seems to have bitten into the 'wicked witch's apple' and fallen asleep for hundreds of years? Or is that its greatest asset? It is certainly one of the most unaltered farm buildings the authors have come across for a very long time-- indeed the whole complex has a strong feel of time having stood still for one generation after another for hundreds of years. The authenticity of this building makes it a remarkable survivor. The problem or, perhaps more accurately, the challenge, is to undertake a scheme of 'high conservation' that results in the preservation of the maximum amount of historic fabric, whilst at the same time giving it a new lease of life as a domestic building providing shelter for yet more generations to come. It needs the lightest and most sensitive of approaches if its full potential is to be realized and the inherent continuity of human endeavour in this part of the world is to be maintained.

Future Thoughts and Possibilities

Noting its historic significance, Little Pool Hall requires a sensitive conservation scheme for its restoration after an in-depth archaeological survey. There is no inherent reason why the farmhouse and its out buildings should not be capable of providing one of the most delightful of historic homes in the principality. Something will have to be done someday; it would be far better to see Little Pool Hall continuing to slumber until the right person comes along than for it to be abused unwittingly by unskilled hands.

Madryn Castle Gatehouse, Boduan

Gatehouse Listing Grade – II
Authority – Gwynedd County Council

Description

All that now survives of the beautiful Madryn Castle is an early seventeenth century gatehouse; a sad reminder of a once illustrious Welsh country house. It was home to the Madryn family from the sixteenth century before passing into the hands of the Jones-Parry family around 1740. Madryn Castle itself was rebuilt nearer the gatehouse during the late 1820s in the most fashionable Gothic style. It seems likely that the gatehouse was probably remodelled in early nineteenth century in an attempt to romanticise it and to add an air of the picturesque to the whole proceedings.

The contents were sold during July 1910 attracting much attention: Madryn formed a veritable treasure trove, with various items being purchased by the National Museum of Wales and the University College of North Wales at Bangor, (now Bangor University). Portraits by Reynolds, Gainsborough, and Hoppner together with a craved mirror by Grinlin Gibbons were amongst the items sold. Unusually, nearly 3000 acres were purchased by Caernarvonshire County Council for £45,000 to create small-holdings. Madryn Castle itself, together with eighteen acres of land was run as farm school. This continued up until the 1960s when the school was transferred to nearby Glynllifon; regrettably, the historic house was demolished following a fire in 1968 leaving the gatehouse as a sad reminder of a once great mansion and family that built it. Today, this forlorn structure lies in ruins in the centre of a holiday park.

The Problem

Local folklore would have it that the last hereditary owner to fully occupy the castle was completely unaware of any impending financial doom up to the point he was given details by his butler. 'Mercy, Mercy!' he apparently exclaimed. 'I am undone. Take me at once to my bed.' It is said that he never recovered, which is hardly surprising if he had known that his ancestral home would one day be demolished, the site become a caravan park and the gatehouse a ruin in its midst.

Future Thoughts and Possibilities

This hugely picturesque and historic gatehouse, could still, with fairly modest resources, be rescued for posterity. A careful conservation exercise with judicious selection of design and materials could form the basis of the renaissance of this remaining fragment of Madryn Castle and the Love-Jones-Parrys, its previous hereditary owners. Even if merely consolidated as a ruin, this fine building should not be lost as the options of a full rescue must always be kept open. It certainly could be an asset within the holiday Park.

Stables Listing Grade – II*
Authority – Conwy County Council

DESCRIPTION

You would be forgiven in thinking that near to these magnificent stables was once built a magnificent country house of the highest order, but Melai is the exception to this rule. No great mansion was ever constructed nearby nor was it ever fully envisaged. Melai had been an important seat since the early medieval period and was the ancestral home of the Wynnes of Melai and Maenan Abbey. From here are descended the Wynnes of Garthewin and the Wynnes of Glynllifon and Rug.

Never more than a gentrified farm, it reached its apogee during the late sixteenth and early seventeenth centuries when members of the family took positions as High Sheriffs for Denbighshire. During the early eighteenth century, it seems that Melai was tenanted and run as an estate farm. What survives today is a particularly fine stable and coach-house built in 1804 to serve an unrealised dream to rebuild the ancestral seat by the Newboroughs; their crest can still be seen on the weathervane on top of the cupola. It formed in essence a model farm, yet did not serve any great house nearby.

THE PROBLEM

This lovely, symmetrical stone stable block would grace any large rolling eighteenth century parkland in England, yet here it is seemingly isolated on its own narrow valley in a quiet part of North Wales, not far from Abergele. The accompanying house was never built and the old house was never gentrified. For a long time it was effectively an exquisite set of farm buildings for the surrounding holding, which has since been sold separately. In some respects, therefore, Melai stables resemble the proverbial beached whale.

FUTURE THOUGHTS AND POSSIBILITIES

The general standard of workmanship and design is very high and the extent of covered space is considerable. Given the property's quite close proximity to the ever popular Chester and north coast of Wales, these buildings seem to represent a great opportunity for a tasteful conversion to residential use. This is a rare opportunity, as it is infrequent that a property of this quality is so immediately suitable for a relatively easy residential development. Someday, therefore, some group or families will be lucky enough to have their homes in a building of much distinction set in completely unspoilt countryside; how fortunate they will be!

House Listing Grade – II*
Gardens Listing Grade – II*
Authority – Gwynedd County Council
National Park – Snowdonia

Description

Historically famous and of refined proportions, Nannau was described by Thomas Pennant in 1784 as being 'perhaps the highest situation of any gentleman's house in Great Britain.' Ancestral home of the Nanney family and, from the eighteenth century, the Vaughans, the earliest reference to the site dates back to the late eleventh century. Huw Nanney Hen built a grand house which was praised by contemporaries but may have suffered as a casualty of the Civil War. Colonel Huw Nanney rebuilt in 1693; this survives in ruins behind the main house. The estate then passed to a near relative, Robert Hywel Vaughan, who

constructed the present mansion in 1795. Joseph Bromfield designed pavilion wings circa 1805, but these were swept away during the 1960s.

Brigadier C. H. V. Vaughan, the last of the line to occupy the house, opened it to the public, but nevertheless placed Nannau on the market in 1964, together with twelve acres of grounds, for £8,000. Accommodation was advertised as comprising four reception rooms, billiards room, twenty-two bedrooms, squash court and hard tennis court. Proposed uses included an adventure training school! The estate was put up for sale in 1975, but did not sell and is still up for sale in 1975, but did not sell at that time. However, a year later Brigadier Vaughan died. Nannau mansion was offered for £65,000 in 1978 by its then owner David Muirfield. Converted as a public house, it was opened again in the 1980s but failed to attract much business at 700 feet above sea level in the wilds above Dolgellau. More recently, after a succession of further owners, the entire interior has been stripped out except for its fine staircase; every window has been replaced as well as the roof, perhaps somewhat needlessly. We know of no plans having been put forward for its future at the time of writing.

THE PROBLEM

Oh what a problem, enough to make one weep! This was one of the great Welsh estates until just a little while ago, when it was sold off to an inspired owner who thought that its remote location, high in the hills above Dolgellau, would attract passing trade as a pub. This did not last long; what a surprise! The next owner then decided the only way to deal with a dry rot outbreak was to strip out the entire contents: floors, doors, architraves, windows, shutters and plasterwork; inconceivably, the lot went. Brand new windows have been installed and most of the structural timberwork inside is now new. The staircase remains, but what a nightmare for the Local Authority to deal with, and what a ghastly loss for our built heritage. It could have been worse, of course, had the house been lost completely. Even so, none of this detracts from its glorious setting.

FUTURE THOUGHTS AND POSSIBILITIES

There is no reason why the future of Nannau should not again be equal to the glories of its past. It is now not a huge house, with the removal of the service wings in the 1950s, yet the rooms that remain are of delightful proportions and effectively amount to four good reception rooms and as many bedrooms and bathrooms as the new owner would require to the upper floors. What fun somebody is going to have installing credible interiors that pay homage to those that have been lost but without imposing an impossible financial burden on themselves. Perhaps the greatest attraction of this house which is its site and setting, both of which are genuinely breathtaking; one cannot think of any better except perhaps Iscoed in Carmarthenshire.

House Listing Grade – II*
Gardens Listing Grade – II*
Authority – Ceredigion County Council

Description

One of Wales' finest Palladian houses and home to the influential Powell family for over two hundred and fifty years, the mansion was built in 1739 for Thomas Powell M.P. on the site of an earlier building. According to architectural historian Anthony J. Parkinson, Nanteos is one of the few great houses of Cardiganshire to have survived without undergoing major rebuilding in the Victorian period. The architect of the eighteenth century house is unknown, but both William Coultart and Edward Haycock are recorded to have carried some work on the mansion during the nineteenth century. John Nash and his assistant George Repton came to produce lavish plans for the remodelling of Nanteos and surrounding grounds, but it seems that these were never executed. The death of

Edward Athelstan Powell in 1930 brought to an end the male line of the Powells of Nanteos. His wife, Mrs Margaret Powell, lived on at Nanteos for another twenty-two years, keeping together the estate and mansion as best she could. Their only son had been killed during World War One, so there was no direct heir to the estate. Through the courts, a will was proved which had been found lining a drawer in the house and was witnessed by a pair of French nuns who had been housed at Nanteos during World War Two. Mrs Betty Mirylees thus inherited the historic estate and proceeded to open the house to the public. Grant aid was provided for a new roof in 1958 but, by 1967, the inherited 4,000 acre estate had dwindled down to 2,600 acres. Nanteos was thereafter sold to Mr and Mrs

Geoffrey Bliss who continued to open the house to the public and kept everything in good repair. They sold the mansion in 1983 but, after a brief occupancy, the estate passed into the hands of bankers. A renaissance occurred in 1989 when Nanteos and twenty-six acres were purchased by a Mr Gary Hesp who slowly returned the house back to life. In 1999, Nanteos was once again sold and was purchased by a Cardiff based development company that continued to open the house.

The Problem

It is a pity that Nanteos should be appearing here at all, many years after the mansion first came on the market for sale with around 3,000 acres and a most distinguished history, but sadly it has been downhill all the way since then. Poor old Mrs. Powell would have wept to see the estate now after all the sacrifices she made during her day to ensure that the house, contents, and estate continued after her day, but it was not to be. After many years, semi-derelict and ravaged by dry rot, it has of late been used as a bed and breakfast venue, which is fine, but unlikely to point towards a secure future, given continuing problems; the poor state of the chimneys and some parts of the façade necessitating the support of acroprops in front of windows. Whilst the roof was re-leaded at great cost many years ago, sadly this has not prevented the occasional ingress of water into the semi-derelict third floor on account of inadequate roof-level drainage.

Future Thoughts and Possibilities

Fortunately, the house is now in the hands of new owners who, one hopes, will be able to undertake a comprehensive conservation scheme of maintenance, repair and renewal, so that the fabric of the house is safeguarded in a manner worthy of its listing status. It is a wonderful house, with its ancient kitchen fittings still mainly in place and a sumptuous first floor drawing room. By no means is this house too large to earn its living as a family house once again, and we wish the new owners every success in their preservation of what has been called the finest house in Cardiganshire.

Stables Listing Grade – II*
Authority – Ceredigion County Council

DESCRIPTION

Ceredigion's finest set of stables were built during the circa 1830 to serve Nanteos and have been attributed to William Coultart, who was working on the mansion at that time. The main front consists of a Roman triumphal arch which affords access into the stable quadrangle; missing today are statues of a horse and pair of eagles which used to adorn the entranceway and which seem to have been sold during the late 1950s or early 1960s.

A pair of pavilions was built either side of the arch with pilasters, a Greek Doric frieze and blind windows. On either side of the stable yard is a four-bay coach-house with grooms' quarters above. When originally constructed, the stables themselves had stalls for up to twenty-four horses; some of these were later altered to loose boxes, possibly in the 1890s. Today, this fine range of ornate stables is in far worse condition than the mansion house following many years of neglect, yet it remains alluringly complete.

The Problem

If only the problem here was restricted to the absence of Romans in their Togas, but sadly, this wonderful neo-Grecian building is in a desperate state of repair. It appears that no new use has been attempted since the last of the horses and carriages departed. Thus, it is a wonderful survivor of a large country house stable block with its stalls, coach houses and servants accommodation, all largely untouched. By no means has this building come anywhere near to being beyond repair. The most immediate problem, therefore, is to undertake emergency repairs in order to keep options open for new uses whenever there is a realistic prospect of them being identified. One cannot leave this object without congratulating one particular former owner of the house for buying the stables back from separate ownership so that both house and stables have now been reunited – what a hero!

Future Thoughts and Possibilities

A future use for this building that harms its character as little as possible is undoubtedly something of a challenge but, located just a few miles away from the busy university town of Aberystwyth, it would seem that this should not prove too daunting a challenge. One does, of course, have to rely on all involved to come up with innovative lateral thinking that will ensure that these delectable stables are not lost and can earn their own living. We wish the owners well in their search for a fellow traveller who might come up with the necessary ideas to unlock this challenge. There must be a solution in there somewhere – certainly leaving it to fester is not the answer. This is a classic case calling for 'moth balling repairs.'

NEUADD FAWR, CILYCWM

House Listing Grade – II
Authority – Carmarthenshire County Council

DESCRIPTION

Neuadd Fawr, or 'Great Hall,' was first built by William Davys in 1784 – 85 to the designs of W. John of Tally. Between 1828 and 1831 the house was extended and remodelled extensively, possibly by Edward Haycock of Shrewsbury. The eighteenth century, three storey house was essentially extended to the east with three grand reception rooms and a magnificent entrance hall with central cantilever staircase in between. It has been suggested that the extension of Neuadd Fawr in the 1820s effectively introduced Regency/Soanian architecture into mid-Wales, making it one of the regions most important neo-classical houses. A service extension was added to the rear of the house in 1889, providing kitchens and further bedroom accommodation. The house finally left the hands of the Campbell-Davys family during the 1940s, when it was used as a school and then as a youth hostel between 1948 and 1951.

In 1951, the Youth Hostels Trust conveyed the freehold of the mansion and grounds to Grace Edith Campbell-Davys, a sister of the last hereditary owner, who sadly did nothing with the house, even elementary repairs. After her death, it was put on the market again; the house and grounds were eventually purchased by a local farmer. He made an application in 1996 for listed buildings consent to demolish, but this was refused. The house has been recently transferred to a limited liability company to reduce the impact of a possible Compulsory Purchase Order on any of the adjoining farmland. Today, Neuadd Fawr is wholly derelict; nearly all of the floors and ceilings have collapsed. The roof too is in a perilous state, but some original features have survived remarkably well; these include the cast iron entrance porch, some ornate plasterwork and the balconies. It is understood the corporate owner may be willing to sell.

THE PROBLEM

This building comes nearer to heaven than most in Wales, hence all who know it end up grieving whenever the name is mentioned. The site is spectacular and the house was an utter joy before becoming derelict. This could still so easily once again become a house of modest proportions and extreme allure if only somebody would take on the challenge. This may mean obtaining assistance at every feasible level if this house is to be saved. What a shocking reflection on us all if it were to be lost. Needless to say, the house's saviour would need to be a person of gritty determination who would ensure that it commanded adequate setting and had sufficient access.

FUTURE THOUGHTS AND POSSIBILITIES

The rescue of this notable house of innovative design near the head of the Towy Valley is likely to need good will and determination from all concerned. How delightful it would be if it once again became a principle residence and part of the surrounding landscape! There is no reason why it should not as a matter of principle. Most probably all concerned would have to 'give a little' for this to be achieved, but surely there is nothing less than benefit for all concerned if a rescue operation was successful.

Norton Manor

A Case Study

House Listing Grade – II
Authority – Powys County Council

Description

Norton Manor is a large austere stone faced 'Jacobethan' house situated on the edge of its own estate village just north of Presteigne. Sited overlooking an extensive and mature park and surrounded by the remnants of its once large and fine garden and arboretum, the present structure is the product of the Price and Green-Price families. The Prices were minor gentry from Carmarthenshire, one of whom John Price had come up to Knighton in the early eighteenth century to practice as an attorney. By marrying the heiress of his client William Chase, a successful London merchant, he had acquired extensive property near Knighton including the Monachty and Pilleth Estates. It was John Price's second son Richard (1733 – 1797) who

having failed to purchase the Stanage Estate from the Powells purchased Norton Manor Estate sometime between the death of his elder brother Chase in 1777 and his own death twenty years later. The present structure dates from the second quarter of the nineteenth century and has affinities with the work of Thomas Penson (c.1790 – 1859), a pupil of Thomas Harrison of Chester, County Surveyor for Denbighshire and Montgomeryshire and the architect of a number of 'Jacobethan' mansions from the 1830's onwards. Richard Price's nephew, Richard Green Price (later a Baronet) inherited the estate in 1861 but found 'the house gloomy and hidden by old trees', according to his daughter's journal. It was he who cut many back and created the beautiful garden with terraces, archery ground, arboretum and croquet lawn and added a large wing to the house for his extensive family. During the 1870s, the family was at the height of their power and influence and the estates in Radnorshire totalling nearly 10,000 acres were producing nearly £8,500 a year. However, their glory was short lived as the family had to leave the manor in 1883 to live in the village. Dying in 1888 it was his trustees who in 1892 sold Norton Manor by then a massive house and the surrounding part of the estate to the first Baronet's son-in-law Powlett Charles Milbank. Born 1852 in Yorkshire he was a nephew and heir to the large fortune of the last Duke of Cleveland. He too stood as MP for Radnorshire as well as being the Lord Lieutenant and President of the RWAS. On inheriting his father's Baronetcy and interests in Yorkshire he made the latter his home in the years before the First World War, selling Norton Manor and the few thousand acres surrounding it in 1919.

When Norton Manor was advertised for sale again in 1936 it had only two hundred acres left, little more than its park. It was requisitioned in the war and in 1958 the then owner Mr SA Cuffs was granted planning permission for twenty caravans on the former pleasure grounds. A Mr Felton-Smythe subsequently purchased Norton and then sold it on to Mr Edmunds who unsuccessfully sought planning permission for 277 residential caravans and 37 holiday vans, though the numbers there now would suggest that no such permission was declined. During the mid nineteen nineties Norton was sold again, the stables were converted to a residence and the house opened as a country house hotel. Redecoration went on inside without attention to the by then urgent structural failures until the inevitable happened on the night of the 10th/11th December 1997 when the bowing lintel over a ground floor bay window in the south west wing at the rear of the house collapsed. This brought all the façade of the three storeys above it crashing onto the lawns where it still lies. This effectively bought an end to the hotel, an eminently suitable use for the building with its four massive reception rooms and even larger scale hallway. The building now stands hardly used and little survives of the Price/Green - Price/Milbank tenure though there was until a few years ago their armorial glass in the stairway window and the Victorian gravestones of the family pets arranged in the flower bed beside the front door. However there still exist at the end of the park on the Presteigne road the twelve Wellingtonia trees each planted to commemorate the birth of a child of the first Green-Price Baronet.

THE PROBLEM

The house has suffered the usual depredations of being parted from its original family followed by endless owners intent only on cheap commercial exploitation. The house is still a fine one but has been separated from its estate and much of the parkland planting has disappeared, but worst of all the chalet's and caravans have crept almost up to its walls and over the once fine gardens. Any future use of the house will require these to be pushed back or screened. Obviously the fallen façade needs to be rebuilt, though luckily at the moment this does not seem to be endangering the main body of the house, of which it represents only a small portion.

FUTURE THOUGHTS AND POSSIBILITIES

The house needs to find a use either as a hotel or as a private residence in single or multiple occupation. However, such a scheme is going to take a lot of funding given that the house and its setting are so compromised. Although the house won't fall down immediately, as it is substantially built, every caravan and chalet that is added in the vicinity makes a long term solution for the house ever more problematic.

ORIELTON BANQUETING TOWER AND GAMEKEEPER'S COTTAGE

Banqueting House Listing Grade – II*
Gamekeeper's Cottage Listing Grade – NOT LISTED
Authority – Pembrokeshire County Council

DESCRIPTION

Orielton has been inhabited since at least the reign of Henry II although the present day house mostly dates from the early nineteenth

century. Up until 1857, the estate had been in the hands of the same family for nearly seven hundred and fifty years. It was then sold to Mark Anthony Saurin of Cilwendeg, who restored the great house from a state of semi-dereliction. During the mid-twentieth century, the estate was sold again and today functions as a Field Centre. Breathtaking views are the reason why the banqueting tower was situated at the highest point of the park, overlooking the undulating fields which roll out to the coast. Today, the three-storey brick tower from the 1730s is roofless and slowly crumbling away; long gone are the days when it was used for picnics on summer days. All the large, square-headed window casements are missing and the internal plaster has weathered away, together with all the floors and internal fittings. Oddly, the tower is a skewed square in plan but it has been suggested, perhaps fancifully, that the base, which is of rubble stone work, may have originally been built as a lookout tower as at St Donat's Castle in the Vale of Glamorgan.

According to the 2004 SAVE Buildings at Risk catalogue, the Landmark Trust have expressed an interest in this building but their efforts have not yet proved fruitful. The present owner, a local farmer, has expressed an interest to sell and may provide enough land for there to be an adequate setting– not much is needed. Also ruinous is the newly picturesque Gamekeeper's Cottage, which is identical in design to the West Lodge at the entrance for Orielton. The remains of the cottage are substantial and it still retains much of its Gothic detailing as well as the bases for its three octagonal chimneys. These two structures no longer belong to the Orielton Estate but are owned by a local farmer.

The Problem

'Where are you Vita? Come and rescue this tower too!' What a brilliant combination are these two buildings, situated in the delightful Pembrokeshire countryside very close to one another. Both are in disrepair and derelict, but by no means are either in a condition to justify giving up all hope.

Future Thoughts and Possibilities

Both taken together could result in an astonishingly unusual but worthwhile home. Both appear to be relatively sound, so there are no intrinsic problems with these buildings as far as one can tell. But what an opportunity to 'do a Sissinghurst' in Pembrokeshire! There must be someone out there who will take them on at the right figure; there is no need for either of these to be lost to posterity. Alternatively, they could make top quality holiday cottages in a country that seems to be something of a magnet for the discerning tourist.

Church Listing Grade – II*
Authority – Anglesey County Council

DESCRIPTION

What could this be? The upturned hull of a ship washed up on the coast of Anglesey by the battering waves of the Irish Sea? No, indeed it is not; it is far more exciting and unusual. Designed by an Italian architect, Giuseppe Rinvolucri, in a most imaginative way as a Roman Catholic church. Rinvolucri had married a girl from the Midlands, who after contracting tuberculosis in 1930 came to reside in Wales. After her death, Rinvolucri decided to seek ordination and was accepted for training in Rome. He decided, however, that he did not have a vocation and turned to church building, finding employment designing many Roman Catholic churches in and around North Wales. None, however, were as experimental and innovative as Our Lady Star of the Sea.

Highly striking and immensely individual, the church was constructed out of stressed concrete, utilising its plastic qualities to achieve a high domed interior and an exterior representative of the upturned hull of a boat. Continuation of the nautical theme can be seen in the portholes that pierce the roughcast rendered plinth on which the building stands. Internally, Cadw describes 'the ribbing that is such a prominent feature of the exterior... dominates the design of the interior; the body of the church illuminated by bands of geometrically patterned natural light between the ribs. The lateral walls have marble panels which also follow the pattern of the ribs; to the top are paired panels, each with a moulded quatrefoil plaque depicting Stations of the Cross. The marbled panels continue at the far end of the church, raised up over round-headed doorways flanking a recess

painted with a depiction of the crucifixion; star shaped lights follow the line of the domed arch.' Today the church has been closed for worship and no future plans are in place, pending a full refurbishment.

STOP PRESS! We are delighted to record that large public funds have now been allocated to this great building, but of course it remains at risk until work has been completed.

The Problem

This is a paradox. On the one hand it is listed as one of the finest modern churches in Wales, whilst on the other hand it is in disrepair and some structural defects evident. For example, there is some subsidence of long standing to the entrance steps and in some parts the mass concrete structure of the building leaks, but none of this should in itself justify declaring it redundant or beyond repair.

Future Thoughts and Possibilities

As by far the finest modern church on the island, one would have thought that this should have been the last to remain and, indeed, we believe that the Church has reviewed its position in this regard. Furthermore, a pragmatic approach to the structural problems could pay dividends. The first job, therefore, is to obtain a structural report from a conservation engineer who aims at pragmatism. If, as seems likely, the structural problems can be held at bay for another fifty years or so, then why should we worry? Equally, if the Catholic Church cannot be persuaded to continue with the building, then surely there must be some other denomination or social group willing to take it on.

PANT GLAS, LLANFYNYDD

A Case Study

House Listing Grade – II
Gardens Listing Grade – II
Authority – Carmarthenshire County Council

DESCRIPTION

Pant Glas was built on the site of a much earlier house, probably of seventeenth century origin, which was incorporated into the Italianate house devised during the early 1850s by E. L Blackburne of London. David Jones M.P., grandson and heir of David Jones, founder of the Black Ox Bank, Llandovery, had commissioned the new house to match his social standing. Its Italianate and flamboyant architecture echoed Osbourne House on the Isle of White. It seems to have been complete enough by September 1854 when David Jones M.P. was welcomed home to his mansion which had cost around £30,000 to build. It was probably the most sumptuous Victorian house in Carmarthenshire in its day.

Built on a very lavish scale, it was entered via a doorway from the loggia which opened out into a spacious and lofty outer hall which was separated by a triple archway from the main hall. The handsome library opened off this room, fitted with bookcases and casement windows to the terrace. The Eastern Room was next, hung with oriental tapestries and lamps. On the other side of the entrance hall was the drawing room, decorated in white and gold, with marble fireplaces, mirrored panel doors, and a richly ornamented ceiling. Following on

was the boudoir or music room decorated in a similar vein, which then led into the dining room, fitted with a handsome fireplace and carved oak overmantel. The final reception room, the billiard room with its glazed top-light, was fitted with two fireplaces and gave access to the conservatory.

From the main hall, the first floor was reached by a splendid mahogany staircase which opened up to a balustraded gallery with central skylight. There were nine good square bedrooms with dressing rooms, as well as a first floor family drawing room or boudoir. Four further large secondary or bachelor bedrooms opened up from a corridor. Despite its size, there were only three bathrooms and four water closets. On the second floor, via the secondary staircase, were eight servant's bedrooms as well as four attic rooms.

Within the service section of the house, the eighteenth century structure had in the main survived, albeit in modernised form. Before the demolition of the mansion it was still possible to discern the eighteenth century windows. Most unusually when the house was fully functional as a private residence, the service wing was entirely separate and shut off from the family's quarters.

The lofty and large kitchen was fitted with a double gradient range, ovens, dressers etc. The scullery was fitted with hot and cold running water and followed onto the servant's hall, the housekeeper's room, the butler's pantry, china cupboards, lamp room, dairy and larders, store rooms and other necessary adjuncts, while below were the domestic offices of the earlier house as well as the wine cellars.

After the death of the last surviving male heir in 1903, the house was sold to Dean Spence of Gloucester, whose son in turn sold the property in 1919 to Mr Lewis of The Gnoll. It was subsequently purchased by the Local Authority as an asylum which functioned up until 1965, after which it was damaged by fire and left empty. Pant Glas was then sold in 1972 to a private property developer who has subsequently demolished the mansion, except for the tower and a small section of walling. Today, the stable survives intact and is in use as part of the holiday park. Above the archway into courtyard is the date 1851, which supports the date of construction of the house. In the main the gardens survive intact, although not to former standards.

The Problem

The problem at Pant Glas is that it is gone, except for a fragment that has eccentrically and incongruously been allowed to remain. For many years the house was in the ownership of the Local Authority as an old peoples' home; after it had become redundant it was damaged by a savage fire. The loss to the county has been shocking in terms of alternative uses and jobs. But something has been made of the good Georgian stable block and the landscaped grounds that still remain. We have been told that consent to put over one hundred log cabins in the grounds was given on appeal many years ago. Thankfully only a little of this development has been carried out.

Future Thoughts and Possibilities

How these fine fully registered grounds and stables could possibly be thought to benefit from a pile of log cabins is impossible to understand, especially as they would wreck the setting of the stables. Maybe this doesn't matter to some, now that these stables are in commercial use which may benefit from the log cabins, but the bottom line is that forty years or so ago this was still one of the great estates of Carmarthenshire. This is no longer the case; effectively it has been wiped out, seemingly without anyone being willing to make the most of it, as opposed to the least. On the other hand, there is all the potential for the stables to be developed further as a fine hotel, set in grounds that could still become some of the finest in South Wales. This then is the challenge; to conceive a future that does not involve log cabins destroying the grounds, and to make the very most of the very good stable block that remains.

CAPTAIN SUPERINTENDENT'S HOUSE, PEMBROKE DOCK

Building Listing Grade – II
Authority – Pembrokeshire County Council

DESCRIPTION

Built in 1832–4 as the home of the Captain Superintendent of the dockyard, this building is comprised of four bays and three storeys. At the rear is a long wing of stables and a coach house. During the 1930s, the building was used as an Officers' and Sergeants' Mess for the RAF. In the 1960s, it opened up as a hotel which had great success with travellers en-route for the Irish ferry. This closed several years ago and the building lay empty ever since.

Pembrokeshire County Council agreed in 2005 that they would issue a Compulsory Purchase Order for the building if a partner came forward to develop the site, as the owner had not complied with a previous Repairs Notice. However, during the early hours of 8th August 2006 the hotel was set ablaze; fire crews quickly arrived on the scene but the roof and upper floors had come crashing down. There were fears that a night watchman was trapped inside but luckily he had been working elsewhere when the hotel caught on fire. At the time of writing, despite the blaze, the ground floor rooms still retain their elaborate cornices, but it will not be long before water ingress through the partially roofless shell causes them to degrade.

THE PROBLEM

The problem here, quite simply, is that the building has been burnt and there appears to have been no action to stop rainwater cascading in. This is deeply saddening as these buildings generally are of high quality, reminiscent of similar buildings at Sheerness and Plymouth. Thus they are far too good to be written off.

FUTURE THOUGHTS AND POSSIBILITIES

So far as one can tell there is no reason why this building and its neighbour should not be rescued for residential use right away. It is excellent architecture within the old dockland area which could be used as part of a development including these houses renovated as private flats or even houses in single occupation. These could provide fine accommodation at reasonable cost, much to the advantage to the surrounding area. One can do no more than to pass on every good wish for success to those who are interested in taking this problem on so as to be able to have a house of distinction in the fullness of time.

Castle and Gatehouse Listing Grade – II*
Dovecote and Long Barn Listing Grade - II
Authority – Newport City Council

DESCRIPTION

One of the most romantic and spectacular ruins included in this book is the fortified Tudor manor-house of Pencoed Castle. It is thought to have been built by Sir Thomas Morgan during the early sixteenth century on the site of a moated Norman castle that was held in 1270 by Sir Richard de la More and in 1306 by Maurice and Walter de Kemeys. It is possible that some of the Tudor buildings were incorporated into the medieval castle. The Morgan family resided at Pencoed until the end of the seventeenth century, but by 1780 the castle had passed into the hands of the Gwyns of Llanhowell and was subsequently let to farmers. In 1914, Lord

Rhondda purchased Pencoed along with Penhow Castle and proceeded to restore them both with the architect G. H. Kitchen. Work ceased with Lord Rhondda's death in 1918. Lady Rhondda and her daughter eventually restarted the restoration, but this time employed Eric Francis as architect. Lady Rhondda then sold Pencoed by auction in 1931, together with four hundred and twenty-five acres; it was subsequently operated as a commercial farm throughout most of the twentieth century. Pencoed is surrounded by a rectangular moated enclosure with the remains of a thirteenth or fourteenth century curtain wall and one surviving circular tower on the south west corner of the site linking up with the exquisite Tudor gatehouse. The long barn is of sixteenth century date with seventeenth century alterations, although was extensively restored in 1879. Set in a field to the north west of the castle is the dovecote built circa 1600 to serve the manor.

A planning application was put forward in 1990 for a two hundred bed hotel, two golf courses and conference and leisure facilities but was never completed– thank goodness. In March 1998, plans were unveiled for an eight hundred acre theme park to be constructed around the ruins of the castle. It was claimed that 'Legend Court,' as it was then titled, would have created over four thousand jobs and attracted over three million visitors. It was planned to be the first ever undercover, climate-controlled park which would include hotels, a film studio, shops and a giant theme park. The £750 million project was rejected by the Local Authority, and many of the local residents were opposed to such a large scale development on this site. All of the plans were overturned in 2001 when the central attraction, Pencoed, was put up for sale for £2.5 million. It was purchased in 2003 for £1.7 million by a local property developer; plans were unveiled in 2006 for the conversion of the castle into offices with an enabling development of further office buildings and twelve residential properties in

the grounds, but no work appears to have been started so far.

The Problem

In some ways the fact that this building exists at all alleviates the sense of any immediate problem. Sadly, though, it is at risk on account of it having been an empty shell for the past forty years or so. As far as one can tell, on the other hand, there is no reason why this building could not be re-kitted out in an appropriate manner and so become one of the most evocative houses in South Wales. Although one's heart does sink at the thought of it being the focal point of a huge commercial development; that is not heritage conservation as we know it.

Future Thoughts and Possibilities

Even with the most opaque of rose-tinted glasses this is almost unbelievable– a miniature version of Arundel Castle so very close to Cardiff. It is inconceivable that local people have not been falling over themselves to acquire this mighty building as a house of the highest standing. There is undoubtedly some blessed person out there, very possibly reading this, who will one day be the saviour of Pencoed Castle, and the best of good fortune to whomsoever they may be. This is a Welsh opportunity at its best and most exciting.

Plas Coch, Llanedwen

House Listing Grade – II*
Authority – Anglesey County Council

DESCRIPTION

Plas Coch is a rare example of a late sixteenth century country house which has remained relatively intact externally and received sympathetic later extensions and alterations subsequently. The original house was built in 1569 by David Hughes and probably consisted of a single block containing the hall and apartments, with a separate kitchen wing to the side. Some remodelling and the addition of a tower during the 1590s extended the house greatly, introducing a Flemish feel to the overall appearance. A great overhaul occurred in the early nineteenth century, which included that creation of the dining room in about 1820, and again in the late nineteenth century, when the north gable was re-built expertly in the style of the original house. The refitting of the interior was in fact so comprehensive in the 1820s as to warrant speculation of a fire having taken place at that time.

Death duties crippled the Hughes family during the twentieth century, and a large area of Anglesey coastline around Cemaes Bay was given to the National Trust in lieu of payment. In 1958, grants were made available for the house by the then Ministry of Works for repairs but, after leaving the hands of the hereditary family, Plas Coch went through various uses including a night club, bar, restaurant, caravan park and car boot sale venue, etc. Following many years of semi-dereliction and neglect,

STOP PRESS! Since the time of writing this building has been saved. Plas Coch has been purchased by a Leisure Group which has set about creating a holiday home park in the sixty acres of estate left with the house. This will include the building of lodges and hard standings for holiday homes, this aims to be finished by 2009. Work is now well underway on Plas Coch itself for its renovation and conversion to a hospitality center for the caravan owners.

THE PROBLEM

There may not be much of a problem here, since following our visit in 2005, the property has been sold and a full renovation scheme is underway. It is a delightful old house that was in single residential use until fairly recently. Indeed, it can be regarded as one of the great Jacobean stone houses of Wales even though it had a somewhat unfortunate and over-thorough internal makeover in Victorian times. Part of the wider estate has been affected with holiday caravans but this should not necessarily harm the house too much– even though they are not very far away.

FUTURE THOUGHTS AND POSSIBILITIES

Given its fairly modest size, the house could well go back to private residential use and single occupation, or it could change its use to something connected with the caravans and the tourist industry. This may already be in progress, and we can but hope that whoever tackles this building does so with the lightest hand and most delicate touch. Thank heavens it would appear that this building is no longer travelling down the slippery slope of abandonment and ruin.

Plas Dulas, Llanddulas

House Listing Grade – **UNLISTED**
Gardens Listing Grade – **UNLISTED**
Authority – **Conwy County Borough Council**

Description

Built for siblings Elizabeth and John Easthope as a summer residence on the slopes above Llanddulas, Plas Dulas afforded exceptional views out over the Irish Sea and the surrounding countryside. There had been a house on the site since at least the 1820s, but what survives today was reconstructed some twenty years later as a retreat by Miss Easthope on account of her father's remarriage in 1843. Sir John Easthope was a self-made man whose early speculations on the stock exchange reportedly earned him £150,000 in three years; he then entered politics and was active up until 1847. Easthope famously purchased the ailing Liberal newspaper, the Morning Chronicle, from William Innell Clement in 1834 for £16,500 and was created a baronet in 1841 by Lord Melbourne.

Elizabeth's younger sister Louisa married Andrew Doyle in 1843, who had become the editor of the Morning Chronicle. They also settled in Llanddulas in 1852 close to Plas Dulas. This move coincided with a legal dispute over their brother, John Easthope's, will which Elizabeth believed had been destroyed by their father, Sir John Easthope, so that he would inherit his son's estate. Father and daughters had been estranged for nearly three years but the court proved that Sir John had not destroyed the will and wished for reconciliation within the family. Andrew Doyle purchased a small estate called Pendarren, near to Crickhowell, Powys in 1868. Later that year, Elizabeth died at Pendarren House and was buried in Llangenny Church yard. The Doyles took up residence at Plas Dulas, which was their principal residence until 1879 when they transferred to Pendarren. Andrew Doyle's only child, John Andrew Doyle, inherited both estates in 1888 but leased out Plas Dulas. On his death in 1907, Pendarren and Plas Dulas were left to his cousin, Professor Richard Dawkins, Director of the British School at Athens and great-grandson of Sir John Easthope.

Pendarren was then sold off but Plas Dulas was retained. Dawkins took up residence during the first months of the First World War and, up until his death in 1955, would spend his holidays at Plas Dulas. Evelyn Waugh, amongst many other notables, was a visitor and it is said that the house was the inspiration for Llanabba in Waugh's 'Decline and Fall,' published in 1928. The contents of Plas Dulas were sold off by Sothebys; they included a large library and many valuable works of art as Dawkins was a

keen collector. A collection of Mediterranean views by Edward Lear received considerable interest and realised £1,273-- over £100,000 in today's money. The house had also been filled with Egyptian, Roman and Greek antiquities amassed during many years of archaeological excavations, all of which were sold by Sothebys at the same time.

Plas Dulas was then sold twice; first to a Miss Fekete of Hungarian origin who took up residence and stayed there until the 1990s. She died intestate and the house lay empty; a local couple then took up squatters rights, stating they wanted to restore the house but to no avail as relatives of Miss Fekete were found in Hungary and Plas Dulas was put up for sale. During this time no repairs had been carried out, thus allowing the building to slip into decay whilst vandals and thieves stripped items of value away. It was purchased in 2001 for £190,000 by a local developer who had plans for renovation; the building was securely boarded up and sheeting put over the roof but the damage had already been done.

The Problem

Today, Plas Dulas is little more than a shell; various plans have been put forward by but little work has taken place. This again is the sort of property that has been around for so long that it is taken for granted and forgotten. It is a typical coastal residence of North Wales in the sense that it was a holiday home and only fully occupied during the warmer parts of the year. Internally there were nearly sixty rooms including the main house, service wing, coach house and stables. The grounds still extend to several acres and include a private drive with entrance lodge, a walled garden and good old stands of ornamental planting with some tree preservation orders.

Future Thoughts and Possibilities

Despite the neglect, the solid limestone of the external walls are good and in reasonable condition. It is possible that the house was designed by Miss Easthope or her brother themselves, as it is rather eccentric and of an organic nature, being built over several levels. One can hardly say that it is great architecture, but it does form part of the grain and patina of the Welsh countryside just as so many others in this book do. Along one side of the property is modern residential development which may be discretely planted out to allow continuation as a house in single occupation. However, due to the erratic nature of Plas Dulas's layout, division into apartments seems far more likely. Further sensitive development within the grounds could provide free-standing homes and fund the renovation of the main house. This property seems to offer a really worthwhile small development opportunity that could well be accomplished in stages.

House Listing Grade – II
Authority – Wrexham County Council

DESCRIPTION

Once the ancestral home of the Kynaston family, today this proud and dignified house stands graffitied and neglected. The Kynastons had at one time owned nearly all of the land in the parish of Cefn Mawr together with the Lloyds of Plas Madoc. Last occupied as a private house during the 1930s, it was owned by an eminent veterinary surgeon, Professor Share Jones. The house probably dates to the early eighteenth century but was substantially remodelled in the early nineteenth; a fine well staircase with shaped undersides to stone steps, and square balusters is a principal feature of the interior.

Now much reduced in size through the removal of the rear service sections and stables during the mid-twentieth century, the building was used as council offices for many years. The

local library was then housed inside until 1970, when the local council changed its use to a youth club. Last used a playgroup centre, most of the building is now empty except for a few rooms which are used as a gardeners store for the nearby Bowling Green and gardens. Oddly, instead of reusing the historic house, it was decided to build an entirely new library adjacent to the Plas Kynaston. Today, the site is currently under the ownership of the local council.

The Problem

The Kynastons were a large and dominant family in this area. In fact they still are, but sadly no longer live in this wonderful house. Equally sad is that it appears to be marooned in a sea of contemporary dwellings. Not only that, but the public have access up to the front door at the present time and the service wing has been demolished. This, therefore, is quite an intractable problem, which is a pity given that it has for such a long time been a significant part of the life of the area.

Future Thoughts and Possibilities

It is just about possible, with heavy and judicious planning, for the property to revert to some form of residential use, especially as it has reasonable views and the remains of a good garden. Failing this, some form of community use would by far be the preferred option, especially as the house's current plight would appear to have been created as a result of unsympathetic development control. Very probably the future of this historic property depends upon an enlightened approach by the local council; certainly things could be vastly improved from what they are at present.

House Listing Grade – II*
Authority – Gwynedd County Council

DESCRIPTION

Idyllically situated above the Dee Valley with views out towards Moel Emoel, Plas Rhiwaedog's history dates back well into the early medieval period. Rhirid Glaidd is recorded to have lived at Rhiwaedog during the twelfth century when it was called 'Nevadden Gleision' after the blue colour of its buildings. What stands today is mostly of sixteenth century origin, except for the storeyed porch which bears a date inscription of 1644, although on the fireplace inside the house is a date inscription of 1699. From the eighteenth century onwards, Rhiwaedog seems to have been only a secondary home, as the

Lloyd family had intermarried into many of the local great houses; it was offered for sale in 1829 but does not seem to have been sold. It passed sideways to the Prices of Rhiwlas, who rented the mansion out.

Revealingly, during the late nineteenth century a contemporary wrote that the old mansion 'presents a sad picture of dilapidation and neglect, uttering a loud complaint against the ignorance or indifference of the proprietor.' This must have been remedied somewhat as considerable Victorian additions are present presumably following a scheme of restoration and re-habitation. It was put up for sale in 1927, advertised at 'an extremely low price' together with all the oak furniture. There were four principal entertaining rooms as well as sixteen bedrooms, stables and a coach house. After leaving private hands Rhiwaedog was purchased by the Youth Hostel Association who modernised parts of the structure, but in 1997 it was closed down and once again sold on. Today the site is abandoned; all overgrown as the house once again becomes a sad picture of dilapidation.

THE PROBLEM

Were this house to be sited in a lawless part of the world it would be expected that many an aspiring owner would have fought to the death to get his hands on it– it is that good. The area around Bala is known to be stunningly beautiful, and to cap it all is this fine house has its own residential, fortified gatehouse leading to a small internal courtyard in front of the main house itself. Its last use would appear to have been as a youth hostel and the interiors have suffered somewhat accordingly. Equally, it appears to have very little land, but who cares, with a house of this quality in this lovely part of the world! Yes, indeed, money does need to be spent and perhaps liberally, if it is available, but the sooner it is back in occupation again the better, especially by a rescuer who will eventually live in it and love it to distraction. It certainly deserves it to be.

FUTURE THOUGHTS AND POSSIBILITIES

It is only to be hoped that the current owner might share our ambitions for this property in the long run and to have the benefit of occupation for him/her self. It is not too large and should therefore be ideally suited to those with a sense of history, vision and determination. Those that have these qualities will be more than amply rewarded day-by-day during the entire course of their ownership, and indeed may be rewarded by being able to pass it on within the family.

House Listing Grade – I
Gardens Listing Grade –
Authority – Carmarthenshire County Council

Description

Plas Taliaris is a very elegant, early Palladian, Bath stone mansion situated to the north of Llandeilo. Built originally in 1638 by the Gwynne family, some exceptional seventeenth century ceilings survive, comparable locally to those recently lost at nearby Edwinsford. It was refaced and remodelled in 1780 following a forced sale in Chancery to Lord Robert Seymour upon whose death the estate was put up for sale in 1832, comprising 3,200 acres and described as 'forming a handsome elevation, and in every respect adapted for a nobleman or gentleman who wishes to combine a residence with an

investment.' It was sold by the widowed Lady Seymour to Robert Peel, cousin of Sir Robert Peel and a wealthy Lancastrian businessman.

Taliaris continued in the Peel family until 1954, when most of the estate was sold to its tenants. A grant was received from the Ministry of Works in 1958 for some restoration to be carried out on the house when a redundant wing was removed. The mansion was sold again to the Reverend Max Williams in 1967. Plas Taliaris then became a religious retreat and was fully functional until 2006. It was recently put on the market with a local agent with a guide price of £900,000 and seven acres of grounds, and was sold. At the time of the sale very little of the original room layouts survived; however, in the dining room, over the fireplace and above the doorway are two seventeenth century paintings depicting rural scenes which are in good condition.

STOP PRESS! We believe that this property has now been sold for renovation as a single house.

The Problem

'Dearly beloved Carmarthenshire, you do hold some of the most wonderful, intractable problems.' Taliaris is perhaps one of them. This noble Georgian house, with a far earlier core, sits majestically on a hillside in the middle of the county with phenomenal views. But, at the time of viewing it was up for sale and in

much need of a new owner to rectify the many problems that have resulted from years of quasi-institutional use. Many of the rooms have been unsympathetically divided up, there is a long backlog of repair and the gardens are a shadow of what they used to be. In particular, the Bath stone dressing to the façade needs some specialist attention. Indeed, the whole building would benefit from being decommissioned from its institutional feel.

Future Thoughts and Possibilities

This is a very pretty house indeed and, in its day, must have been exceptionally costly to have been built of Bath stone. It is a real ornament of the countryside and thus a delectable family home. There is no doubt that whoever purchases it and undertakes what work needs to be done could well find themselves in possession of a home that will remain in the family for many generations to come, precisely as has been the case in the more distant past.

House Listing Grade – II*
Gardens Listing Grade – I
Authority – Monmouthshire County Council

DESCRIPTION

Overlooking magnificent parkland, Sir John Soane was employed here by George Smith to rebuild the ancient house of Piercefield between 1792–3. Smith was soon declared bankrupt and was hastily forced to sell the unfinished house in 1794, even before the roof was complete. Colonel Mark Wood purchased it and commissioned the eminent architect Joseph Bonomi to erect the pavilions either side of the central block as well as to fit out the now lost interiors. A curved Doric portico was constructed in the centre of the main house and provided a sophisticated, formal entrance to the mansion. Built expensively of Bath limestone ashlar on the exterior, the interior walls are made up of brick; all vestiges of internal decoration have fallen away or been removed. Some bas-reliefs do, however, remain in the pavilions but they are in a perilous condition.

Piercefield passed through the hands of several families until 1923 when it was abandoned and sold to the Chepstow Racecourse Company who established horse racing in the park there in 1926. Degradation of the house continued up until the Second World War when Piercefield was requisitioned; however, the American troops stationed in the grounds used the old mansion for target practice! Despite nearly ninety years of neglect, Piercefield has once again been placed on the open market with approved plans for the full restoration of the house. A price tag of over £2 million has been attached to it together with a substantial portion of land; thankfully the Local Authority have stated that no extensive enabling development would be allowed as the essential setting of the mansion is integral to the concept of the site.

THE PROBLEM

There are two fundamental problems here: first, the house and its pavilions are roofless shells and second, even in this condition, they represent some of the finest architectural statements at risk in Wales. The house is not very large– so what a crying shame that it has been allowed to get to this condition! At least many options have been kept open and one must commend the owners of the racecourse for putting the property on the market for sale so that it can be rescued. There is an obvious temptation for new owners to approach the interiors in a manner that is unnecessarily lavish, which in turn can upset budgets. On the other hand, all involved should recognise that this is one of Wales' premiere houses, where short-term economic funding factors should not entirely be the predominant consideration. Pragmatism could be the order of the day, and let us not forget the service quarters of such properties formed a large part of them, though this is no longer so. We can, these days, perhaps do without much of the space required for such domestic functions so that the main reception rooms should now claim a far higher percentage of the total cost than in the past.

FUTURE THOUGHTS AND POSSIBILITIES

Private domestic use in single occupation is clearly the best possible use for this property and we hope that the selling owners will persevere until they get the right purchaser with the right funding. Likewise, we would suggest that intending purchasers should concentrate mainly on the rescue operation and not on short-term economics. A 'boutique hotel' could also be a very worthwhile solution. Certainly it will sell some time provided the vendors keep their nerve.

House Listing Grade – II*
Authority – Denbighshire County Council

DESCRIPTION

This site originated as a medieval deer park, one of five belonging to nearby Ruthin Castle. A house of substance has been established here since at least the sixteenth century when, in 1617, a certain Thomas Needham of Pool Park is recorded to have served as High Sheriff of Denbighshire. Thereafter, the estate became a possession of the Salisbury family of Bachymbyd and Rug, and thence passed through marriage to the Bagots of Blithfield in Staffordshire in 1670. The present house and its associated estate buildings were laid out between 1826 and 1829 for the second Lord Bagot, to designs by the architect John Buckler, possibly in collaboration with Benjamin Gummow. The Bagots retained the estate for less than a century afterwards.

The staircase is the finest element of the interior, with panels depicting cherubs in combat with sea-monsters and biblical scenes alternating with strapwork panels. The balusters are rich with allegorical figures and angels.

By 1919, Pool Park was tenanted by Sir Ernest Tate, Bart., the sugar magnate, who served as High Sheriff of the county in that year; however, within a decade it was sold again. In 1937, the house became a convalescent home and subsequently a psychiatric hospital, serving as a branch of the North Wales Mental Hospital at Denbigh. Since the 1990s, the building has been empty and the interior is affected by both dry and wet rot.

The Problem

Whilst this was a secondary house for the Bagots of Blithfield in Staffordshire, it still held its place amongst the great estates of Wales for many centuries. Parts of the ancient house have survived, but were subjected to a reasonably competent Victorian makeover with some very high-quality stonework. It is not a huge house but has remained empty and unused since the mental patients left over ten years ago. They were there for many years but fortunately did not add much that could not now be removed with relative ease. Dry rot is undoubtedly a problem, as it is in most houses that have lain empty for a while, but the major problem for us all is that this fine item of the Welsh heritage is at risk because it is not occupied and loved as it was in the Bagot's day. Urgent action needs to be taken to halt the dry rot and then to 'moth ball' the house so that all future options can be kept open.

Future Thoughts and Possibilities

With judicious demolition of some of the ancillary buildings, this lovely house could so easily become a family home of distinction with about ten bedrooms and an appropriate number of bathrooms. The gardens are still there and just need to be brought back to life. This could become a great opportunity for someone capable of issuing and controlling a number of contracts consummately in order to bring about the building's resurrection. Are we really a nation that has so lost its imagination that we cannot come up with a family that is eager and able to breathe life back into Pool Park? Surely not! But equally right action is needed to stop further deterioration.

House Listing Grade – II
Authority – Monmouthshire County Council

DESCRIPTION

Usk Priory was once home to an Order of Benedictine Nuns, and was connected with the adjacent Church of St. Marys. Following the dissolution of the monasteries during the 1530s, the building was acquired by the Jones family, who resided there from about 1555 until 1810. Upon the death of the last member of that family, it was then sold to the Dukes of Beaufort of nearby Troy House. In 1865, the eighth Duke of Beaufort sold the Priory to Thomas Watkins of Highmead, Monmouthshire who in the event did not own it for long, as a Mr. Robert

Rickards then proceeded to buy the house from the mortgagees of Watkins in 1888.

Today the Priory is in a sorry state following a savage fire which caused much damage to some portions of the interior. Part of the property is currently used a storage yard for salvage materials. Also on the 'at risk' register is the pretty gatehouse which forms the principal entry point to the Priory and retains much of its historic fabric.

The Problem

It would appear that the problem may not be so great, for here is a house of much distinction, excellently sited next to the parish church in one of the foremost towns on the border with good views over surrounding meadows. It has had some unfortunate internal alterations over the years, but then few houses haven't. This perhaps is part of the fun of a rescue operation; working out what is to be kept and venerated, and what is to be dismantled and removed. It would appear that lack of adequate repair over the years is all that is really wrong with this house. It is a joy to behold, on lower ground next to the church, just waiting for sympathetic and appropriately-skilled conservation. It should therefore be a relatively easy exercise to bring the necessary skills and finance to bear upon this house at the same time.

Future Thoughts and Possibilities

In some ways, this fine house fits the description of an idyllic ancient home better than most. There should therefore be no reason why the sadness of seeing it with holes in the roof should not be alleviated by professional conservation-based renovation well before it actually starts to fall down. For most of us it represents an ideal opportunity for conservation as a comfortable family home; let us hope that someone else sees this well.

Scheduled Ancient Monument
House Listing Grade – II*
Gardens Listing Grade – II*
Authority – Caerphilly County Council

DESCRIPTION

This is one of South Wales' most important buildings at risk; it is also one of several houses built by prominent courtiers of Elizabeth I and James I during the early seventeenth century on advanced designs influenced by visits to Italy. Sir Thomas Morgan had married into the Lewis family of Ruperra who had been established there since at least the fifteenth century. By 1626 he undertook the complete rebuilding of Ruperra, whose design is that of a transitional property from the medieval military architecture to that of the Italian Renaissance. Robert Smythson, one of the famous architects associated with this particular design is complimented by John Thorpe whose Book of Architecture contains a design very similar to Ruperra. Its four corner towers are echoing nearby Caerphilly Castle and also Plas Teg in North Wales, built by another wealthy courtier. Lulworth Castle in Dorset is perhaps the most similar to Ruperra

with its circular corner towers and centralised entrance ways; it too was burnt out, but has now been rescued by English Heritage and is open to the public.

A fire in 1785 resulted in considerable internal and external alterations by Thomas Hardwick. The gabled dormers were replaced with battlements, which may have been possibly due to fire damage. Ruperra remained with the Morgans of Tredegar who continued to live there well into the twentieth century. The fortunes of the Morgans had declined by 1935 and the three thousand acre Ruperra estate was the first part to be put up for sale. It failed to sell and the contents were sold over a three day sale. Later, whilst under requisition by the army, a fire caused by faulty wiring occurred in 1941 and gutted the interior. The Morgans then sold all of the Tredegar estates in 1956 which included the ruins of Ruperra. Following a succession of different owners and little maintenance, the integral structure of Ruperra deteriorated rapidly; in 1982 part of the south-east tower collapsed after developing severe cracks. It appears that other towers may face the same fate. In 1998, the castle was sold to a local businessman who has submitted plans for the conversion of the main building into nine residential flats together with an enabling development of eighteen houses in the immediate grounds, causing uproar locally. A building preservation trust is currently campaigning for the restoration of the castle.

The Problem

This problem property has become something of a cause célèbre in Wales. It is almost identical to Lulworth Castle in Dorset which is one of the jewels in the crown of English Heritage: yet precisely the reverse is true of this equally great castle at Ruperra. Like Lulworth it suffered partial death by fire but unlike Lulworth it still is still a roofless shell. Nothing whatsoever has been done to stabilise the ruins, nor has any other work been attempted in order to keep options open for future generations. It is a tragedy for Wales that this has happened. Sadly, it has passed through several hands over recent years and is now the subject of an inappropriate planning application which if approved will destroy the historic setting of the very building it purports to save. Poor, poor old Ruperra, not so long ago one of the great domestic castles of Wales, yet now it is being picked over like some long-dead horse in the desert. What a tragedy for Wales, but what an opportunity for an enlightened and determined owner.

Future Thoughts and Possibilities

Unbelievably, Ruperra is little more than a bow shot away from Cardiff city centre and in all common sense should have been redeveloped for residential use many years ago. Even now there is no reason why a sympathetic development scheme should not see the huge areas of outbuildings and the castle itself converted to modern use in a manner that scrupulously respects its past and adds to its future. Let us not forget that Ruperra is a hugely important item of the national heritage of Wales which becomes more at risk day-by-day. Yet as a nation we do little more than watch this part of our heritage die. We are all to blame in one way or another. Let us hope and pray that there is in the great 'out there' someone who will come along and take our chestnuts out of the fire in this instance. An agreed planning brief (i.e. agreed by Cadw, the amenity societies and the local trust) would be a welcomed start to the process.

Building Listing Grade – II
Authority – Gwynedd County Council

DESCRIPTION

Also known as Llwyn-y-brain, this pretty, early nineteenth century house has breathtaking views over Caernarfon and the Irish Sea. Dr. John Hughes M.D., a naval surgeon, bought the demesne in 1808 and proceeded to build, incorporating the old farmstead as a bakehouse for his newly acquired estate. Improved during the 1850s, Anglesey Marble fireplaces were fitted together with a porch and the exterior was stuccoed. Sir Goronwy Owen, Liberal Chief Whip and MP for Caernarvonshire, purchased the estate in the 1920s and proceeded to add piecemeal, so the estate consisted of about seventy acres by 1957.

A dental practitioner from Caernarfon then bought Llwyn-y-Brain as a family home and lived there for about thirty years. In 1986, the estate was acquired by a Mr and Mrs Evans who restored and converted the stables into the Seiont Manor Hotel. Their interest was then sold to Leading Leisure Hotels, Virgin Hotels and, most recently, Hand Picked Hotels. Llwyn-y-Brian itself is not used and stands derelict to the side of the thriving hotel, waiting for a new use to come along and wake this sleeping beauty!

The Problem

Doubtlessly some readers in Gwynedd, when coming across this name, will wonder why we appear to be listing a thriving hotel as an item of heritage at risk. And there is the rub; these are in fact two entirely different buildings, but sharing a similar location and name. In some ways it is rather sad to think of a brand-new hotel adopting the name of a nearby country house, whilst the former thrives and the latter decays. It would appear that the hotel was constructed from a nucleus of farm buildings that once formed part of this estate and which presumably were converted when redundant to the farm use. It has to be said that this has been undertaken with a high degree of sympathy and is certainly not the sort of intrusive structure in open countryside that one normally associates with such developments.

Future Thoughts and Possibilities

Although this is not a huge house, it could indeed make a truly wonderful home whereby the hotel could be a distinct advantage to it. Sadly, though, this fine little manor house with excellent views appears abandoned and at risk of dereliction. Fortunately, the hotel is sufficiently far away so as not to dominate the manor house or to harm its principal views. There is no reason, therefore, why the manor house could not, tomorrow, become a comfortable, even luxurious family home of considerable appeal. Alternatively, there would appear to be no reason why it could not contain some form of hotel facility provision. But in any event it should not lie fallow as it is indefinitely.

SHIRE HALL, HAVERFORDWEST

Building Listing Grade – II*
Railings, Gates and Steps – II*
Authority – Pembrokeshire County Council

DESCRIPTION

Designed by William Owen, four times Mayor of Haverfordwest, and completed in 1837, in a handsome classical style. Giant Ionic pilasters appear to support the central pediment of the facade and internally too pilasters form an integral element, lining the semicircular rear wall of the main courtroom, which has a remarkable coffered barrel ceiling through which daylight is nevertheless allowed to enter. The iron railings which survive in front of the building are also by Owen and were probably manufactured in the town's own foundry. The Shire Hall occupies a prominent position in Haverfordwest, dominating the High Street and Castle Square in the heart of the town.

Yet it has stood empty, unused and steadily decaying since May 2000, when the magistrates' court made a long anticipated move into more modern quarters. In 2002, Pembrokeshire County Council confirmed what had long been rumoured in the town, that the building was to be sold. The announcement proved highly contentious given the Shire Hall's history as a place of entertainment as well as a court of law, and the fact that the town was ill equipped with public meeting spaces.

Over many months, in the face of protests and petitions, Pembrokeshire County Council conducted negotiations with a nation-wide chain of public houses. Other interested parties included local groups who hoped to use the building for the benefit of the community and as a tourist attraction. By this time the attraction of the Shire Hall had been augmented by the fact that the successful bidder could expect, besides the building, the sum of £317,000 which had been earmarked under a major townscape renovation scheme. Nevertheless, at the eleventh hour, the publicans abruptly withdrew. There followed a hiatus during which Pembrokeshire County Council remained adamant that the only solution to the Shire Hall problem lay in its sale to a commercial organisation. At the end of 2006, Shire Hall was sold to a local property developer who has proposed installing an estate agent's office, pizzeria, and of using the courtroom for auction sales. There has been little movement since.

The Problem

Several years have elapsed since the Justices departed and, although some heating has been installed, the Shire Hall remains damp and visibly deteriorating. Very little has been spent on its maintenance leading to an area of plaster falling from a ceiling in one of the upstairs rooms. Yet it is still a joy to behold, nestling at the bottom of the hill leading to the great church of St. Mary's; the problem therefore is finding a new sympathetic use that will carry this building well into the 21st century for the benefit of the town and its visitors.

Future Thoughts and Possibilities

The obvious solution here is to find a use that does not compromise the essential character of the building as a whole, particularly its dramatic and impressive interior. Just like many redundant churches, banks and building societies with similarly important interiors which have quickly attracted alternative users we do not expect that this building will remain on the at risk register for long.

Banqueting House and Grotto Listing Grade – II*
Shell House Listing Grade – II
Authority – Flintshire County Council

DESCRIPTION

Talacre was once the home of the Roman Catholic branch of the Mostyn family. A house is recorded to have been on the site since 1634, but the only certifiable building prior to the 1820s rebuilding of the main house is an eighteenth century banqueting house. Sir Edward Mostyn commissioned Thomas Jones of Chester to design a new house which is the present day Talacre Hall. The Mostyns sold the estate in 1920 to a closed order of Benedictine nuns, who added a church to the main building, opening out of the former private chapel which was integral with the main house. In 1988, the nuns left Talacre for the former Ursuline Convent, Curzon Park, Chester. After Talacre fell afoul of vandals, thieves and neglect, a local dentist purchased the building as a family concern but little work was carried out on the building. The surrounding gardens, which included the buildings at risk featured in the book, were sadly and inexplicably sold separately from the main house. The main Hall's fortunes finally turned for the better when a local businessman with a passion for historic buildings won a neck-and-neck race to buy it and then put a great deal of commitment and resource into restoring it and its immediate grounds as a private house in an exemplary manner.

The beautiful banqueting house is said to have been designed by Capability Brown and is situated within the former kitchen garden of Talacre. Palladian in style, it is an exceptionally rare structure and forms part of the integral components of the landscaped garden. Thankfully, a temporary roof has been placed over the structure to prevent further dereliction. An exceptional set of garden features can be found in the wilderness that surrounds the oasis of Talacre Hall; a folly shell tower and artificial rockwork grotto, contemporary with the mansion, with shell decorated rooms, connected by corridors covered with motifs and grotesque imagery. A dragon with a hole for its mouth can be seen in one wall; a fire could be lit so flames and smoke emerge, much to the delight and fright of the guests! Hopefully, these unusual early nineteenth century pleasure gardens will one day be restored back to their former delight.

THE PROBLEM

It is amazing and saddening as to the quantity of talent, refinement, intelligence, imagination and funding that was required to create one of the great estates here, and conversely also saddening how such fabulous heritage could subsequently be so little cared-for. Talacre Hall is a case in point with a distinguished late Regency house and all that went with it in terms of stables, home farm, riding school and sumptuous gardens containing a banqueting house and utterly delightful grotto. The Mostyn family, the hereditary owners, gave up all these allurements 'between the wars,' and ownership of the core area has been most regrettably divided many times as a result.

FUTURE THOUGHTS AND POSSIBILITIES

A particular sadness, even a paradox, is that the house now appears for the first time in ages to be thriving under its new private owner, yet the gardens have been separated away from it and are in a state of utter dereliction. This is a great pity as there appears to be little future for what was a garden of great distinction having any hope as an amenity for the house. The future, therefore, for the banqueting house and grotto appears to be bleak unless reassembly with the main house can be brought about; surely common sense can prevail here for the benefit of the national heritage! By comparison, a rescue operation for the stables in this much sought-after area should be simplicity itself, with the residential option probably being the easiest. Surely if the shell house at Cilwendeg can be rescued so successfully, then so can the shell house here!

House Listing Grade – NOT LISTED
Authority – Carmarthenshire County Council

DESCRIPTION

A much smaller version of North Wales' Hafodunos, Tegfynydd is perhaps the most ornate Victorian gothic house in Carmarthenshire. Its ruinous interior retains many original features such as encaustic tile floors, an ashlar cantilevered staircase and a hooded stone chimney. In the centre of the house was the main hall with a Gothic cathedral-like arcade which was galleried and may well have contained a skylight in the roof. At the rear of the house is preserved the earlier building which may be late eighteenth century in date but was used as the service wing by the Victorian household.

Tegfynydd was rebuilt out of limestone for Howard Spear Morgan in 1873–5, possibly by F. R. Kempton, and was turned into two big canted two-storey bays which are asymmetrical. A local newspaper from 1874 recorded that a stone mason died after falling from the scaffolding whilst involved in the 'extension, restoration and beautifying of the old mansion.' It was last inhabited during the late 1940s, when the then-owner decided to move abroad. For many years the house was neglected and the valuable components such as the lead on the roof was removed, together with a bath carved out a solid piece of slate and stained glass panelling. The estate was divided up and it was only recently that all the buildings have been reunited. Around twenty years ago, the house was put up for sale for £20,000 by a new owner but without much the surrounding land. The offer actually was for the purchaser to take down the building stone by stone and rebuild it elsewhere. Several people sought to buy and remove the hooded stone fireplace but, thankfully, the owner refused to allow it to be separated from the main house.

The Problem

It was with an open mind and neutral emotion that we approached this property for the first time via the adjoining farmyard. How quickly, though, all of this changed! This house is a joy, which could easily be the house of either Trollope or the Warden. It could so easily have been sited in a cathedral close. Why, oh why, did we allow it to become a roofless shell so recently, when it could have made such a delightful home of high Victorian comfort. Sad to say, a modern bungalow has been built just a little too close, but nevertheless far enough away so as not to undermine the possibility of a rescue operation.

Future Thoughts and Possibilities

Of course the bungalow could be re-sited elsewhere if absolutely necessary, though it is doubtful that it is really essential to do so. In any event, there is nothing on the face of it to stop somebody with a will, imagination and funds from rescuing this astonishing survival. It would make a home of the utmost distinction, especially on account of its formulaic layout.

House Listing Grade – II*
Gardens Listing Grade – II
Authority – Ceredigion County Council

DESCRIPTION

Trawsgoed, the principal country house of mid-Wales, was the seat of the Vaughan family for nearly eight hundred years. In the thirteenth century, there was little more than a farm on the site; it was not until 1547 that the estate was vastly increased in size through marriage. By the early seventeenth century, Trawsgoed had become the largest estate in the county. Sir John Vaughan rebuilt the house following damage by Parliamentarian soldiers during the Civil War but, by 1756, it had been refaced in plain eighteenth century style with an L-shaped wing to the north end. Wilmot Vaughan, the 1st Earl of Lisburne of County Antrim, Ireland, further modernised the house in the 1760s and 1770s. It was at this time that the name 'Trawsgoed' was anglicised to Crosswood, a name which would be used until 1947. In 1804 the house was described as being 'altogether neglected…and in decay,' the refronting of Trawsgoed may date to the early 1800s and the 3rd Earl.

Further works were carried out during the 1830s by the 4th Earl who had inherited in 1831; these included the spectacular library with its ornamental plasterwork and the dining room. The portico on the main front also dates from this period. A large service wing was proposed in 1874 by Szlumper & Aldwinckle but was deferred until 1891 and replaced the eighteenth century wing to the right of the original house in the French sixteenth century style. When the 7th Earl inherited the Trawsgoed Estate in 1899, it consisted of over forty thousand acres although his trustees needed to sell some agricultural land to provide working capital and to retain the core of the estate. Maple & Co. of London redecorated the library in the French Empire style in 1900 with strong colours and much gilding, so making it one of the great rooms of Wales, no doubt much appreciated by the then Prince of Wales on a visit in the 1920s.

In 1947, the 7th Earl sold much of the state for £50,000 to the Ministry of Agriculture as the Welsh headquarters of the National Agricultural Advisory Service, which is when the house was adapted for offices. At this time, around 25,000 acres remained, of which 9,000 were sold to agricultural tenants. The 8th Earl of Lisburne inherited the remainder in 1963. The house was reacquired by the Vaughan family in 1996, under the terms of the Crichel Down Rules. Trawsgoed was then transferred to a company in which the family were minority shareholders, which converted the 1891 wing into five apartments and developed outbuildings and parts of the grounds in 2001. A large office/laboratory building built by the university was commendably demolished at this time. Unfortunately, the core of the house was savaged by dry rot and large portions of some interiors were removed, being left 'moth-balled' and unrestored. In 2005, the core of Trawsgoed was put up for sale with Savills and a price tag of £1.5 million.

STOP PRESS! We believe, at the time of writing, it has been recently sold to a new private owner, who is eager to bring about its full rescue.

The Problem

Here again we come across one of the great estates of Wales which simply failed to survive the evolution from the old world to the new. Yet the architectural heritage aspect remains. It is nevertheless always sad to see such property devoid of its hereditary owners and thus at risk of division, the ravages of time, the climate, and the treasury. The old house was not particularly large, dressed as it is in a sombre Georgian way and adorned with the family's coat of arms. But, oh my goodness, what made the reasonably-sized house almost unmanageable was a huge and rather inappropriate Victorian wing. What a shame this could not have been demolished and perhaps the family returned to its ancient home in the Cardiganshire hills. But it was not to be.

Future Thoughts and Possibilities

At the time of writing and on the occasion of our last visit, the property was obviously at risk, with the earlier section of the house partly stripped on account of dry rot. On the other hand, the extent of that risk is now not so great, as the Victorian wing has been converted into apartments and we believe that the old part of the house has recently been sold to enthusiastic new buyers. There is reason therefore to expect that this great Cardiganshire house will shortly come off the buildings at risk register and settle down to a new and secure future as the home of enthusiastic and dedicated new owners.

TROY HOUSE, MITCHEL TROY

House Listing Grade – II*
Gardens Listing Grade –
Authority – Monmouthshire County Council

DESCRIPTION

This is our front cover property; Troy is one of Wales' finest late seventeenth century country houses. Originally the site of a medieval manor, a house was constructed during the sixteenth century which was greatly enlarged between 1682 and 1699 by the addition of an imposing classically-designed main range by Henry Somerset, 1st Duke of Beaufort, for his son and heir, the Marquess of Worcester on his marriage. The sixteenth century house had been the property of the Herbert family, descended from an illegitimate son of the 1st Earl of Pembroke. At the end of the sixteenth century this was sold to William Somerset, 3rd Earl of Worcester, whose successor Edward Somerset, 6th Earl and 2nd Marquess of Worcester, soon afterwards bought the manor of Great Badminton following the ruination of Raglan Castle during the civil war, to which Troy subsequently became subordinate. Edward Somerset's son Henry, president of the Council of Wales, was created 1st Duke of Beaufort in 1682; with Raglan in ruins he built the present mansion at Troy as the family's main residence in Wales.

The estate remained in the Somerset family until 1901, when the Troy lands, amounting to some 1,670 acres, were auctioned off, although the house itself was not sold at that time. In 1904, the Sisters of the Good Shepherd took possession of the Troy for use as a convent school;, and subsequently, with financial assistance from the Home Office from 1935, as an Approved School. The school closed and the house was privately purchased about twenty years ago. Dry rot is now profuse and the plasterwork and great broad sweeping staircase are decaying. The future for this very important building is not certain as no future use has been determined, although some tentative, as yet inappropriate, plans have aired from time to time for residential development around the main building.

THE PROBLEM

The paradox inherent in this house is that it comes close to being a palace, although it is not huge. Nevertheless, it is perhaps one of the most important country houses in Wales, both in itself and in its associations. Now, though, it is in a thoroughly sad state and in considerable disrepair and with little maintenance having been undertaken for a long time. We believe that it has been exposed to the market for sale from time to time, but it would appear that no interest has been forthcoming. Of course, the property market in east Wales has been transformed over the past few years and there is no reason why previous marketing problems should necessarily repeat themselves in the future.

FUTURE THOUGHTS AND POSSIBILITIES

Undoubtedly, Troy is grand enough in every respect to justify a return to private residential use either in single or multiple occupation, although it is likely that the best solution for the house will only come about through wide professional marketing by those who have the expertise and experience in such matters. Whilst this may well provide the ideal answer, there is the ever-present danger of an owner seeking 'boom or bust' through enabling development that would do more harm than good. Given the existing size of the house, it is to be hoped that both planning and listed building consent would only be given for minimal extensions to that which is already there, in a manner that would not affect the essential appearance, character and setting of Troy House. It is difficult to over estimate the cultural importance of this great building.

Listing Grade – II
Authority – Neath Port Talbot Council

DESCRIPTION

A classical house of circa 1800, this building has been overzealously restored during the late twentieth century. During the mid-nineteenth century, it was the home of Mr William Jones and his daughter Jenny, who was an accomplished harpist and who won a prize at the Cardiff National Eisteddfod in 1883. She is reputed to have painted panelled doors inside the house with murals. Following the departure of the family, Tyn-yr-Heol became a ladies' seminary but has been unoccupied for many years. It is made up of five bays, with a detached derelict stable block and an 'in and out' ecliptic

driveway. When up and running there were three reception rooms, a kitchen with larder and pantry, five bedrooms, a bathroom with two water closets on the first floor and four further bedrooms on the second floor.

In 1995, Tyn-yr-Heol was purchased by a local developer who proceeded to build modern housing behind the old house; this did not greatly infringe upon the integrity of the house itself. Little work was done to Tyn-yr-Heol and the house slowly decayed. Tragedy struck, however, when the property was subsequently ravaged by fire; the original roof with dormer windows and tall brick chimneys have gone but an attractive curved porch leading into the house has survived.

THE PROBLEM

It is difficult to put one's finger on the underlying problem here; in most neighbourhoods a fire-damaged house is quickly and uncontroversially repaired and put back into full use in a short space of time. This hasn't happened here. It is a house of some distinction with its in-and-out drive and villa proportions within an established residential area. Even the stable block has managed to survive, though it is admittedly roofless. But this is just the sort of house that

a local prosperous businessman or professional would be expected to take over as a family home of real comfort and some elegance. Indeed, every town and village needs to be able to offer this sort of accommodation if it is to function in a traditional manner.

FUTURE THOUGHTS AND POSSIBILITIES

On the face of it there should be no problem putting the roof back on, the floors back in and once again it could be of valued use for residential purposes in either single or multiple occupation. Here is a great opportunity for someone to do it justice and, at the same time, remove a blighted item for the benefit of the surrounding residents. It should be a case of 'win-win' for all concerned.

WHITSON COURT, GOLDCLIFF

Listing Grade – II*
Authority – Newport City Council

DESCRIPTION

Built for William Phillips circa 1750, Whitson Court has been attributed to the eminent architect John Nash. It seems to have been near completion in 1795 and was complemented by landscaped grounds. The pavilions either side of the main house were respectively a dairy and stable block also of red brick and contemporary with the house. Internally, one of the most impressive features is the cantilevered stone staircase which sweeps up to a circular balcony and glass oculus which apparently is leaking into the house.

Owned by a Mrs Maybury from the 1930s until her death at the age of ninety-nine in 1998, a zoo operated here for many years finally closing in the 1980s. A local man then purchased the house but, despite plans for restoring it to a private house, the house was allowed it to fall into disrepair. During the autumn of 2007, the building was sold privately again to a Newport businessman who is currently restoring it as a private home.

THE PROBLEM

It is so important in this instance, as in many others, that one recognises the only real problem here: a very elegant house in disrepair. There can be no question as to its inherent beauty; that is self-evident. The site and setting have not been compromised and the location is excellent, being near the M4 motorway and only a short drive from Cardiff, Newport, Bristol and Bath. How so many must think of us as an odd lot to allow a housing asset of such great quality to lie fallow. Shame on us all.

FUTURE THOUGHTS AND POSSIBILITIES

This need not be an intractable issue. It just needs someone with a cultivated eye, heroic determination and a deep pocket to metamorphose this pile of dereliction into one of the most elegant of homes in the principality. Certainly not everybody could do it, but an awful lot can if they're prepared to make the opportunity for themselves. Indeed, we have reason to believe that the house may recently have 'fallen on its feet' with a new owner who gives every indication of being exemplary custodian. We wish him and his family every good fortune in rescuing what is not for them the sweetest place on earth! Well done and good luck!

Gazetteer

6 and 6A Spring Gardens, Haverfordwest

House Listing Grade – II
Authority – Pembrokeshire County Council

Built around 1839 for William Rees, Spring Gardens is part of a terrace of seven large two-storied stuccoed houses. The most notable feature is the two-storey veranda of wrought iron, probably made at Haverfordwest's Marychurch Foundry at the time the houses were built. In the large grounds behind is the derelict rockwork grotto. It is to be hoped that a recent sale might ensure the long-term survival of this remarkable property.

10, Old Market Street, Usk

Building Listing Grade – II
Authority – Monmouthshire County Council

Owned by a public house on the same street, this eighteenth century town house was recently council offices but was shut down due to health and safety issues. No action has been taken for at least ten years and it is now not wind nor weather tight. Planning permission has recently been granted for conversion, but action has yet to have been taken. This could be ideal as a single, substantial residence in the delightful Monmouthshire town of Usk. One of the prettiest features of the main front is the fanlight which retains its original Georgian glass.

Gazebo, Pembroke Town Walls

Gazebo Listing Grade – II
Gardens Listing Grade – II
Authority – Pembrokeshire County Council

On top of the remains of a medieval circular tower stands an octagonal gazebo, magnificently situated along the walls of Pembroke's defences. Despite recent modern alterations, the pebble-dashed building retains its Georgian sash windows, albeit without glass, as well as its curved slate roof, topped off by a ball finial. Beneath the facing, the structure is made out of brick and is probably contemporary with the construction of No. 111, likely for Dr John Powell during the early eighteenth century. As far as one can tell, the problem here is little more than one of disrepair which should not lead to the loss of the building over time. Surely, the ideal use here is that of a gazebo, and one would hope that all relevant authorities could exercise their charm, good-will and maybe a modicum of public funding to ensure that the building is put back into good repair. In the long term it would be such a shame if this building, prominent though it is, were to be lost simply through sheer indifference of all those who have a finger in the pie.

Aberpergwm, Glynneath

Building Listing Grade – II
Authority – Neath Port Talbot County Council

An ancient seat of the Williams of Blaen Baglan, Neuadd Pergwm as it was called, was celebrated by bards in the fifteenth and sixteenth centuries. The house was extensively remodelled in about 1850 with crenulations and was further extended in 1876 for Morgan Stuart Williams, who added a new, neo-Elizabethan front range and an enormous long gallery on the top floor. It was then leased as Coal Board Offices during the twentieth century, as they mined the park. During the latter half of the twentieth century,  the house was abandoned and today it is has been badly vandalised and looted, acting as a playground for the local youth. On the other hand, there is enough masonry remaining to form the basis of a fine and unusual house for those with aspiration in this area. It may not happen, but it is worth a try.

Avallenau Stables, Haverfordwest

Stables Listing Grade – II
Authority – Pembrokeshire County Council

 Situated on higher ground to the rear of Avallenau House, the stables command a great view over Merlins Bridge towards Haverfordwest. The main house was built in 1845-6 by William Owen for Williams Evans, solicitor of Haverfordwest. During the later twentieth century, Avallenau House was purchased by the County Council used as a children's home. Recently, it has been refurbished as offices but the stables are still sadly ruinous, yet they provide a great opportunity for rescue as either offices or even as a private house. They should not be allowed to disappear.

St. Baglan, Baglan

Church Listing Grade – II
Authority – Neath Port Talbot County Council

An early, one-aisled chapel in the grounds of a large Victorian new-built church, St Baglan has been out of use for over one hundred years. This historic structure could easily be re-roofed or consolidated for a number of uses such as a community centre, or to residential use, providing rental income or even as a memorial garden for cremations. One would certainly hope that every effort would be made to ensure that this little church is not lost; it will be if nothing at all is done.

Bala Town Hall

Listing Grade – II
Authority – Gwynedd
National Park - Snowdonia

Dear Bala, one of your children is in distress: please help! Oh dear, this fine, wonderful building in Bala seems not to be loved, yet it makes a huge statement in the main street. The worry here is that the costs of a rescue operation increase exponentially as years of neglect are allowed to accumulate. We don't for one moment expect this building to be lost, it is simply that the more time it takes for a rescue operation to begin, the bigger the rescue operation has to be, and the more historic fabric is lost. **STOP PRESS! It is covered with scaffold, so hopefully will be rescued.**

The Bay, Tintern Parva

Building Listing Grade – II
Authority – Monmouthshire County Council

An enchanting cottage, a stone's throw from the majestic ruins of Tintern Abbey. Situated opposite the former Abbey mill, it was possibly the miller's house and detached cottage dating to the seventeenth century. During the mid-nineteenth century, the cottage was remodelled and enlarged and has not been altered since. This makes it a very rare example from the period and it is of special interest for its prominent and well-preserved historic character within the village of Tintern. The building has been disused for some years and there has been a small collapse at the rear of the property, causing it to be no longer wind and weather tight.

St Buans, Boduan

Church Listing Grade – II
Authority – Gwynedd County Council

The former Boduan parish church is now de-consecrated and for sale. It was remodelled to designs by Henry Kennedy and P. S. Gregory of Bangor in 1891-4 for Frederick G. Wynn of nearby Boduan at a cost of £7,000. Cadw have stated that this is an impressive cruciform Romanesque design, a style unusual at the time, though being revived in the Celtic countries. Offers over £150,000 are being sought. This building really ought to remain in some form of religious use.

Bromfield House, Mold

Building Listing Grade – II
Authority – Flintshire County Council

A pretty mid-nineteenth century villa in the suburbs of Mold, which was known to have been occupied in 1871 by William Beale Marston, proprietor of nearby Bromfield Colliery and a local oil works. Elaborate bargeboards relieve the main elevations and add an air of elegance to the house. Apparently, Bromfield still retains many of its original internal features which make it a rare survivor amongst our number. At the time of writing, work seems to be under way to secure the structure following a long period being empty.

Bryn Deunydd

Building Listing Grade – II
Authority – Conwy County Council

This eighteenth century farmhouse gushes forth with charm and history. It was probably built by John Roberts, as his initials and the date 1715 appear in plaster relief in the former parlour. Roberts is recorded as having died the following year. The vicar of Llannefydd, Richard Ingram, appears to have rented the farm between 1737 and 1739 from the Roberts family. In the nineteenth century, the house passed to the Heaton and finally Garn estates. Sadly, as with many old farmhouses, it has been become redundant and a new house as been built nearby. Let us hope it could be saved for use as a holiday cottage of real quality.

Caerau, Church Bay

House Listing Grade – II
Authority – Anglesey County Council

To us, this property is yet another a jewel in the Welsh countryside representing the continuing evolution of a gentry house without any swagger or pretence. Indeed it is in such a state of repair that one would be forgiven for thinking that the family had remained there up until the last ten years or so. Yes, it is in disrepair, but not terribly so and there is no reason why it could not quickly be rescued as a fine family home. It is in the ownership of the local authority, who appear to have little interest in it and have allowed one wing to be effectively abandoned over the last forty years with little or no maintenance. What a great opportunity there is here for the local authority to sell off this wonderful home to a new caring owner who could rescue it, hopefully by the most sensitive of conservation schemes. This would then enable the local authority to provide the local tenant with a new farm house nearby. Potentially, therefore, this is a 'win-win' situation for all concerned.

Caerwent House, Caerwent

Building Listing Grade – II
Authority – Monmouthshire County Council

Prominently sited in the centre of Caerwent, adjacent to the remains of the Roman temple, Caerwent House may have been built on the site of the Roman Basilica. Structurally, it is probably late sixteenth or early seventeenth century in date; most of the house was rebuilt in the early nineteenth century. Today the house is in very poor condition with parts open to the elements. Nevertheless, in these days of great shortage of housing this represents a fine opportunity to acquire a delightful home with good historic associations in an excellent location.

Calcott Hall, Llandysilio

Building Listing Grade – II
Authority – Powys County Council

Built around 1725, Calcott Hall was constructed out of red brick with dressed stone quoins in the early Georgian style. Today, there survives an octagonal timber lantern with glazed sides which crowns the hipped slated roof. A structural survey was carried out in 2003 which showed that the building was still stable, yet little work has been undertaken since then to stop the rot. One of the principal surviving features of the interior is the staircase which is apparently still intact, but for how long? This building must not be lost.

Carmarthen Royal Infirmary, Carmarthen

Building Listing Grade – II
Authority – Carmarthenshire County Council

Built in 1858 by William Wesley Jenkins, it had been founded some eleven years earlier in 1847. The exterior is stuccoed Italianate style with channelled pilasters and a pedimented door case. The main façade is of seven bays with two storeys and a hipped roof. This is an important building and central to the history of medicine in West Wales, yet inexplicably it has been allowed to fester. This should not be allowed to happen - the worthy people of Carmarthen deserve better.

Carreglwyd Semaphore Tower, Llanfaethlu

Building Listing Grade – NOT LISTED
Authority – Anglesey County Council

It would be right to say that this is not far short of a pile of stones, and yet it is so important as an element of national security communications in times of yore. It would be a shame if it were lost and one would hope that the local authority may consider the current structure as a nucleus for perhaps a holiday cottage or some other building so to as ensure that what is left has some sort of future. It certainly has delectable views.

Circular Cockpit, Conwy

Building Listing Grade – II*
Authority – Conwy County Borough Council

This is almost impossible to photograph, but it is one of a handful of such buildings in Wales that should under no circumstances be lost. The current building preservation society owner has stripped the roof and made the walls weather tight (with much grant aid of public funds) as a temporary measure, pending reconstruction of the roof and stabilisation of the walls. So far so good, but when, we wonder, will work begin in earnest to fund the reinstatement works which are so urgently needed? We wish current owners and the local authority well in their efforts to secure this remarkably rare building for future generations. But first of all they need to get to grips with a campaign for fundraising.

Cleifiog Fawr, Valley

Building Listing Grade – II
Authority – Anglesey County Council

This structure was built by the illustrious Baron Hill estate during the first quarter of the nineteenth century, although there has been a farmstead on the site since at least 1730. This fine building is sadly at risk and one hopes that the owners will be able to rectify the situation either on their own or with others before serious damage is done. As for us, we can see there is nothing to prevent it going onto the market for sale right away– perhaps even tomorrow!

Denbigh Hospital, Denbigh

Main Building Listing Grade – II*
Other Buildings Listing Grade – II
Authority – Denbighshire County Council

Built in 1842-8 by Fulljames & Waller of Gloucester, Cadw state that this is one of the most important purpose-built mental hospitals in Wales and ranks as one of the most sophisticated and pioneering of the Victorian asylums in Britain. The buildings are designed in the Tudorbethan style in the form of a U-shaped complex with male and female patients segregated. The hospital went out of use during the mid 1990s and has been recently bought by a property developer for conversion into residential housing. It is very much a cause célèbre, and may be on the market yet again for sale. Someone needs to take this property more seriously in future than appears to have been the case in the past.

Falcondale Coachhouse, Lampeter

Coach-house Listing Grade – II
Authority – Ceredigion County Council

Now a prospering hotel, Falcondale was built for R.Hart Davis between 1812–19. It was rebuilt in 1859 in an Italianate style for the Harford family. The coachhouse and stable court were shown on the 1844 tithe map as a four sided structure but was probably altered after 1859 to coincide with the rebuilding of the main house. Essentially, the problems here are little more than problems of maintenance and repair. We have included this building for many reasons, not least of which that it demonstrates through its simplicity and function the grain and patina of the Welsh

countryside. It also demonstrates the variety of problems that remain unsolved, even sixty years after a great estate was broken up into a thousand little pieces. Thankfully the main house seems to be well cared-for as a hotel, although even here great care needs to be taken if ever there was a call to extend the property to provide more accommodation. So often one has seen similar situations to this where a good country house has been seen as no more than a key to unlock a planning consent for extensive development in the heart of the countryside which otherwise would never have been allowed. In this instance, the problem of disrepair to the two buildings in question is a very minor issue at the present time, but this could escalate if nothing further is done to arrest the problem in the foreseeable future.

Gaerwen Windmills and School Rooms, Gaerwen

Building Listing Grade – II
Authority – Anglesey County Council

The school rooms were erected in 1849 in the Gothic revival style together with the Church of St. Michael when there was a growth in population in the local area. This was brought about by both an influx of workers to the nearby coal mines and the building of Thomas Telford's new road across Anglesey. It was then that the National school was established at a cost of £766 on land donated by the Marquess of Anglesey. Surely somebody could now do something with it, and one would ask a similar rhetorical question in respect of the two windmills nearby; is it a lack of endeavour that is the basic issue here?

Goodig House, Burry Port

House Listing Grade – NOT LISTED
Authority – Carmarthenshire County Council

Originally a farm, Goodig House was the home of the Owen and Thomas families and may have seventeenth century origins. A date stone of 1701 is within the house but no survey has been carried out to ascertain what remains of the earlier building; Edwardian alterations may mask this. During the 1960s through to the 1980s, Goodig was used as a hotel; since then the house has fallen into dereliction.

Great House, Llanhennock Fawr

Building Listing Grade – II
Authority – Monmouthshire County Council

Most of what we see today dates to circa 1600, albeit there are records which state the original farm was built in 1520 by John Morgan. A fire in 1900 led to the refurbishment of the house but not its rebuilding. It is an important gentrified farmhouse which has fallen on hard times; the roof is slowly falling into disrepair and it will not be long before the interiors suffer as a result. This house is on the cusp of becoming a building at risk. A sheet or two of tarpaulin could make all the difference in the long run between loss and rescue.

Great Milton

House Listing Grade – II
Authority – Newport City Council

To the west of the village, up a steep hill, lies the Tudor house of Great Milton. It is an L-shaped, two storey building with an inhabitable attic, its earliest part dating to the mid-sixteenth century. There are early seventeenth century additions and alterations such as the windows when the taller cross range was added. Many early features survive including seventeenth century wooden windows, fireplaces, chamfered ceiling beams and a broad timber newel staircase which led up to the attic. This is an unmodernised and important sub-medieval farmhouse which is crying out for a loving conservator.

Grove Place, Denbigh

House Listing Grade – II
Authority – Denbighshire County Council

Grove Place, formerly the police station, is a mid-late eighteenth century town house. The splendid façade consists of a sandstone plinth, with chamfered quoins to corners and Venetian windows to ground. During the 1840s it was home to Richard Roberts Esq., Mayor of Denbigh in 1847 and 1848. After its closure as a police station, work began in 2004 to renovate the building back into use as a private house; unfortunately, at the time of writing this has long ceased to be the case. What a tremendous opportunity this represents for a clever developer or determined private individual.

Gwaelodygarth, Cyfarthfa

House Listing Grade – II
Authority – Merthyr Tydfil County Borough Council

Richard Crawshay erected Gwaelodygarth for his son-in-law Benjamin Hall: the man who is believed to have lent his name to Big Ben! Built around 1809, it was then rented from 1815 to a son of an Ironmaster in Hirwaun. On Benjamin Hall's death, the house was then rented by William Crawshay the Second until he moved to Cyfartha Castle in 1825. Since then there has been a variety of owners before being opened in 1950 as training school for state registered nurses and remaining with the NHS until 2002. Tragically on 14th August 2003, most of the house was gutted by fire, although planning permission has been granted for housing development within the grounds. It's almost 'odds on certainty' that little action will be taken for this building to survive. Shame on us all if this becomes true.

Hafod, Nantcwnlle

House Listing Grade – II
Authority – Ceredigion County Council

Situated half a mile south of Nantcwnlle, this late eighteenth-century gentry house was built by the Rogers family, later of Abermeurig. It was purchased by the Bishop of David's during the first half of the nineteenth century where it was used to house the Vicar of Llangeitho. The building is constructed from plain stone of three stories with a rather pretty Gothic stair light at the rear. Today, the house is securely boarded up but the gardens show evidence of landscaping which are now very overgrown. The outbuildings are in a state of decay. Potentially, it could be a delightful family home once again. The surrounding area is one of the most magical in Wales.

Hawkesbury Hall, Buckley

House Listing Grade – II
Authority – Flintshire County Council

Hawkesbury Hall was built in 1801 by Jonathan Catherall, an industrialist, philanthropist and leading local non-conformist. The house was named after Lord Hawkesbury, who introduced a bill into Parliment that Dissenters could register a room in their premises for worship. Catherall rode up to London immediately on horseback and registered his room as a place of Dissenting Worship, so it is one of the earliest Dissenters meeting places in North Wales. Today, the park has been turned to public use and a community centre has been built adjacent to the house. This building should not be allowed simply to sit and fester.

Henblas, Brynford

House Listing Grade – II
Authority – Flintshire County Council

A finely situated farmhouse, set high above the Dee estuary, overlooking the Wirral. Dating to at least the mid-seventeenth century, an inscription above the main door reads 1651. When originally listed in 1962 it retained many original features, including a Jacobean staircase. Today, the site is under development yet the house, fire damaged and empty is in a perilous condition. It therefore needs urgent action to keep options open for an indefinite period whilst adjoining problems are sorted out.

Hendre House, Llanrwst

House Listing Grade – II
Authority – Conwy County Council

I am not in the least bit ashamed that this listed building at risk is in fact my home! I have now renovated the roof, parapets and chimneys and indeed live in the service quarters. In some ways, therefore, I do not consider it as at risk, although it could be argued the other way until the main part of the house has been finished, probably within the next couple of years. Nevertheless, it is an utter joy 'to have and to hold.' My bones will rest here some day. Michael Tree

Highmead, Llanwenog

House Listing Grade –
Authority – Ceredigion County Council

Originally built for Herbert Evans in 1777 by John Calvert of Swansea, Highmead has been radically altered and extended from the 1860s onwards. The façade is one of the largest for a country house in Ceredigion and is most impressive when viewed across the Teifi valley. Today the house functions as a private school for foreign children but is in need of much work to prevent it deteriorating further; it is in disrepair. This is a very large house and it would appear that institutional use is right in the long term assuming it is properly maintained.

St Jerome's, Llangwm

Church Listing Grade – II
Authority – Conwy County Council

A church was first recorded at Llangwm in 1210 and much of the present structure dates back to the medieval period. However, currently the building was subject to a mid-eighteenth century re-fenestration and alteration, followed then after that by a thorough late nineteenth century restoration. St Jerome's is now redundant with many of its original internal features including wall monuments now not in situ. The church appears to be relatively weather-tight but for such a historic building, a suitable alternative use ought to be found. It is a very important building right in the centre of this charming remote village.

Leeswood Dovecote, Leeswood

Listing Grade – II
Authority – Flintshire County Council

Probably built during the 1720s, this rather stylish brick dovecote with stone quoins has the remains of a pyramidal roof that is unfortunately missing its cupola. Today, this building is in separate ownership from Leeswood Hall for whom it had been originally built. It is only to be hoped that all concerned can cooperate together to ensure that this building is not lost in the long run. A prime motivating force is needed.

Llawhaden House, Llawhaden

House Listing Grade – II
Authority – Pembrokeshire County Council

Llawhaden had been the home of the Skyrme family from the early 1600s before being gutted by a fire in May 2000 in which the owner also sadly perished. The interior was of sixteenth and seventeenth century date, and included a seventeenth century staircase and a panelled room of similar date. The rear service wing is earlier and contains a barrel vaulted room which mostly escaped the fire. Across the road from the house is the walled garden which contains a ruined gazebo and cistern house. It is to be hoped that this property will be reinstated in the long run by some brave and adventurous soul, whether that be the current owner or someone else. It is certainly worth the time, trouble and expense.

Llechwedd-Llyfn

House Listing Grade – II
Authority – Denbighshire County Council

A delightful farmhouse built high above the upland village of Cerrigydrudion on the edge of the Denbigh Moors, Llechwedd-Llyfn probably dates to the mid-sixteenth century and has survived remarkably well, avoiding any major alteration or addition. It was abandoned in the 1940s but, despite this, has retained much of its roof and interior. Cadw have stated that, despite its present condition, it is an important survivor of a sub-medieval type of construction employing crucks. This could easily be returned to a private house or even a small holding once again; even a distinguished holiday cottage is possible. But it should not be lost in any event.

St Luke's Church, Abercarn

Church Listing Grade – II*
Authority – Caerphilly County Council

One of the most striking inter-war churches to be built in Wales; it was designed by J. Coates Carter, architect of Cardiff and Penarth, between 1923 and 1926. It sadly became redundant in the 1980s and the interior was stripped. It however, retains a strong looking concrete arched roof as well as a lofty tower of rough stone. A local developer has gained permission to convert the church into 9 residential flats with houses within the curtilage. Perhaps not the best of uses, but at least one that will save this good building if the development takes place.

Malpas Court, Malpas

House Listing Grade – II
Authority – Newport City Council

Malpas Court was built 1836 – 8 by T.H. Wyatt for Thomas Prothero of Newport who was agent to the Morgans of Tredegar. It is built of rock-faced Pennant sandstone, with dressed Bath stone and is of two storeys. During the twentieth century it was converted into flats but has still retained much of its character. Today the house is much compromised by the encompassing housing estate which has taken over much of the landscaped parkland. It has been badly vandalised and partially gutted by fire. Yet it could still have a sustainable future in the long term by those who care. STOP PRESS! This building is currently under restoration.

Mostyn House, Vale Street, Denbigh

House Listing Grade – II
Authority – Denbighshire County Council

Despite many alterations and changes of use, Mostyn House still retains much of its eighteenth century character and fabric. As the name suggests, it was a town house of the Mostyn family whose armorial shield still remains above the main door. The building is empty at present, but was expected to be converted into flats in 2005; sadly this has not materialised.

Nant-y-Fridd

House Listing Grade – II
Authority – Denbighshire County Council

Nant-y-Fridd is a typical early nineteenth century farmhouse with an integrated cart bay, stables and hayloft, and including associated dairy outshut and brewhouse. The buildings have been empty for a number of years but have not suffered too badly despite the neglect. One of the greatest problems has been a stream which runs parallel to the house which has burst its banks. This farm has great potential to be a beautiful family home or even a retreat or therapy centre. The possibilities are endless as the setting is excellent.

Newcastle Court

House Listing Grade – II
Authority – Powys County Council

Newcastle Court is a dramatically situated Regency mansion set on steeply-banked terracing and was the seat of Major John Whittaker, High Sheriff of Radnorshire in 1809. Primarily built in the early nineteenth century in the Regency style with picturesque influences, it was altered in the late nineteenth century when pierced barge boarded gables and a Gothic arched door was added. For many years, the previous owners lived in the adjoining service section whilst the main house fell into decay following a legal dispute. It has recently changed hands and thankfully its restoration is currently underway. Another forgotten house making a triumphant return and long may it continue and be completed.

The Observatory, Hubberston, Milford Haven

Scheduled Ancient Monument
Building Listing Grade – II*
Authority – Pembrokeshire County Council

One of the most unusual buildings to be included in this book are the ruins of Charles Greville's octagonal observatory from 1805. It was possibly designed by William Jernegan and was intended as the nucleus of a 'College of King George III' but seems to have been abandoned shortly after Greville's death in 1809. Cadw states that this is a very early example of a masonry observatory dome with slit openings but these have fallen mostly inwards due to disuse. As so often is the case the real problem here is that there appears not to be an obvious use for the building. It is unlikely that this building would be appropriate in the public domain so its future is dependant upon some use being found of it to justify the maintenance costs. It is currently at risk. Not so long ago properties like this really had very little discernable future. However, with the huge increases in price of virtually any sort of building, then surely, if adequately marketed for whatever may be an attractive figure, some form of beneficial use should be obtainable. Much care would need to be taken over the selection of the lucky applicant to ensure that solutions were real rather than daydreams. Just lying here seems to be no solution– at worst it should be taken into the care of Cadw.

Old House, Llangristiolus

Building Listing Grade – II
Authority – Anglesey County Council

Now used as a store and farm shed, Old Bodrwyn was built around 1700 but was superseded by the newer house in the latter part of the eighteenth century, when it was used as stables and servants' accommodation. Cadw states that it is an example of a minor gentry house which includes a projecting rear stair turret, a rarity on Anglesey. It has recently changed hands and the main house is now being restored. However, the old house is still being used as a stable as no other solution has been put forward. This must not be allowed to disappear.

Pencaledog, Caergeiliog

House Listing Grade – II
Authority – Anglesey County Council

This property is very close to the A55 but is in its own way a joy and has attractive outbuildings to the rear. Although the large windows at the front elevation indicate that the house has to a point been compromised, this is something of an illusion as for the most part recent alterations have been few. It would appear that there is no reason why this house could not have a good future in the right hands. Maybe something for the first time buyer?

Pentre Mawr, Trelawnyd

House Listing Grade – II
Authority – Flintshire County Council

A rather provincial and vernacular house, dated 1708 and a late example of mullioned windows, Pentre Mawr forms a delightfully unique property. The house is uninhabited, and probably has been since the erection of a late twentieth century bungalow on the north side of the farmyard. This could be easily be returned to use as a private home.

Pen-y-Bont, Mold

House Listing Grade – II
Authority – Flintshire County Council

Apparently for sale at the time of writing, Pen-y-Bont is situated alongside the river Alyn and reached by a track from the west end of the bridge at Pentre. In origin a row of late seventeenth century single storey cottages converted to a two storey farmhouse in early nineteenth century. Its proximity to Mold and ease of access to cities such as Liverpool, Chester and Manchester, Pen-y-Bont is crying out for a sympathetic owner who is looking for a challenge that will ultimately return dividends!

Plas Chambres Secondary House, Denbigh

House Listing Grade – II*
Authority –Denbighshire County Council

Formerly the home of the now extinct Chambres family, this delightful and historic house originated as a late medieval five-bay domestic block of full-cruck construction. Its juxtaposition with the main house suggests that it was always a secondary unit, and may have originally served as a steward's or dower house. In the late sixteenth century the building was turned into a storeyed house and extended. The building was encased in brick circa 1680 and is now used as an outbuilding for storage. Plas Chambres could become the most beautiful guest accommodation for the main house or as a holiday-let to generate a healthy income to assist its upkeep.

Plas-y-Coed, Port Penrhyn

House Listing Grade – II
Authority –Gwynedd County Council

This structure was built in 1878 as the agent's house to Penrhyn Estate, a use in which it remained until the Second World War. It was until recently a residential home for the elderly, run by Gwynedd County Council, but is now up for sale. Plas-y-Coed replaced Lime Grove, a classical villa of 'chasteness and technical' purity, built by Samuel Wyatt. This is a large Victorian house that could make fine flats or remain as a home in single occupation.

Plymouth House, Llantwit Major

House Listing Grade – II
Authority – Vale of Glamorgan County Council

Dating to the late fifteenth or early sixteenth century, the outward appearance of Plymouth House is that of a seventeenth century building in the early Renaissance style. It was historically owned by the Stradling family of St. Donat's Castle. Today, the house has been divided into two; the right hand side has been recently sold but the left, more derelict section, is still up for sale. Ideally, the whole property should come back together to create one of the most impressive and historic residences in Llantwit Major. With a little luck, this should not be a long term problem given the general attraction of the Vale of Glamorgan and the demand for good houses from Cardiff.

Pwllycrochan Coach House, Colwyn Bay

Coach-house Listing Grade – II
Authority – Conwy County Council

Pwllycrochan was an early nineteenth century mansion built by Lady Jane Silence Erskine as the replacement for an earlier house. The house was further extended in 1840, but was sold by the family in 1865 and opened as a hotel which successfully operated up until World War II. The coach house (maybe part of the Erskine building phases) was greatly extended at various points during the late nineteenth and twentieth centuries. Today, the old mansion and outbuildings are occupied by a private school but since the mid 1990s the coachhouse has had no proper use, decaying slowly over the years. The school are considering demolition so that a new nursery could be built on the site; one hopes that this will not come about and that every effort will be made to save these historic buildings.

Ruthin Castle Medieval Remains, Ruthin

Scheduled Ancient Monument
Castle Listing Grade – I
Authority – Denbighshire County Council

Begun in 1277 at the same time as Flint and Rhuddlan castles, following a brief interlude the building work continued in 1282 under the direction of Master James of Saint George. Today, the ruins of the Medieval castle are in very poor condition and in need of much consolidation of the sort seen at Conway castle and others. Given that this castle saw the start of the Glyndwr rebellion and is central to Welsh history, one would expect all concerned to ensure that these walls are safeguarded in the long

term. This is, after all, one of the most sensitive archaeological sites in Wales.

Siamber Wen, Trelawnyd

Listing Grade - II
Authority – Flintshire County Council

This is a late sixteenth or early seventeenth century house originally composed of two units. It was extended in the eighteenth century and altered to suit contemporary taste, when sash windows were inserted under wedge lintels in typical Georgian style. The house has been uninhabited since the 1960s when the entire roof was blown off during a storm and the family moved to another house close by.

Tan-yr-Allt, Bangor

Listing Grade – II*
Authority – Gwynedd County Council

Owned by Bangor University, Tan-yr-Allt is one of the most
important Georgian buildings to survive in this University
town. The former park is now covered by a night club,
the student's union, university departments and car parks.
Built in 1755 for John Ellis, Archdeacon of Bangor, a
principal feature of the interior is a Chinese Chippendale
staircase. It really is sad to see such a distinguished building
so unloved in the centre of a university.

Woodlands House, Malpas

House Listing Grade – II
Authority – Newport City Council

Woodlands House, formerly known as Malpas House, dates to
the late 1820s and faces the park for Malpas Court. It is two-
storeyed, rendered and has a coach house at the rear. Today, it is
divided up into flats but little maintenance work has been carried
out to prevent the structure from deteriorating. The setting is
compromised and directly in front of the house is the busy
A4051 and a foot bridge from which the photograph was taken.
Nevertheless, one would hope that, with due attention to repairs,
it would be possible for this house to survive in the long run.

Wynnstay Colliery Winding House, Ruabon

Scheduled Ancient Monument
Building Listing Grade – II*
Authority – Wrexham County Council

This structure was built as a vertical winding engine house built
1855-6 as one of the original structures of the Wynnstay Colliery.
It remained in use until the colliery closed in 1927 but subsequently
the machinery was removed and the roof and chimney demolished.
This really should not be at risk at all; consolidation of the masonry
is the very least that should be done right away.

Acknowledgements

From Michael Tree

My first vote of thanks is to my co-author Mark Baker, who so readily volunteered to be my 'runner' when I first mentioned my idea of writing such a book. He has since undertaken much of the research, as well as metamorphosing into project manager. Were it not for his talent in gentle cajoling, this book would probably have remained just a daydream, given my very busy life with amenity societies and another ruined house and garden of my own to rescue.

Undoubtedly the earliest and most fundamental influence was Mrs. Rosemary Rooney of Llwyn-y-brain in Carmarthenshire, who virtually single handedly rescued her own family home from the derelict, barbed-wired ruins in which I often played as a child. Her quiet determination, inspired vision and architectural talent all those years ago enabled her to return to live in her home, against all the odds. This has led many to emulate her achievements, myself included.

I also owe a significant debt to the Dyott family of Lichfield, whose tenacity as landowners and kindly good sense as friends have been examples of good stewardship for me. Finally, I have to thank my late father who, when I was about sixteen said 'If you cannot dream dreams, you will never find your future.' When commenting upon my suggestion of taking on the rescue of Neuadd Fawr. How right, therefore, in this context is the saying that 'Yes, difficult projects take time, and impossible projects take a little bit longer!' The essence of this book therefore is to demonstrate that very few ruins are really beyond hope: perseverance is all.

Joint Acknowledgements

Adam Goodison
Adam Wilkinson
Antoinette Mackeson-Sandbach
Auriol, Marchioness of Linlithgow
Brian Mival
Cardiff Library Service
Carmarthen County Museum, Abergwili
Carmarthenshire Record Office
Ceredigion County Council
Christopher Thomas
Colin & Penny Seaford
Dafydd Lloyd Jones and the North Wales Hospital Historical Society
Darren Devine
Denbighshire Record Office
Dr. Manon Williams
Elaine Davey
Eric Salt
Flintshire Record Office
Gary Cooper
Geoffrey Foster and Haverfordwest Civic Society
Gordon Sharratt
Graham Holland
Graham Jones and Family
Gwenda Griffith

Gwynedd Record Office
Harry Thomas
Harry Williams-Bulkeley
Holly Nicholson
Dr. Ian Dungavell
The late Ian Grant
Ian Lang
Jan Talbot-Jones
Janet Wilding
Jeremy Rye
John Martin Robinson
John Prior Morris
John Thorneycroft
Julio Soriano & Khalil Khairalah
Louis de Wet and Gabriella Drake
Margaret Nicholson
Marilyn Lewis
Matthew Williams
Michael Grime
Mike Roberts
Mrs Cornelia Bayley
Myfanwy Jones
National Library of Wales
Nigel Bowen-Morris
Pat Moseley
Philip May

Professor Sion Fowcs-Williams
Professor Tom Pritchard
Rhyl Library Service
Richard Broyd
Richard Suggett and Penny Icke of the Royal Commission of Ancient and Historic Monuments in Wales
Richard Watson
Robert Bargery
Robert Wall of Cadw
Sarah Ash
SAVE Britain's Heritage
Simon Wardle
Suzannah Fleming and The Temple Trust

Marcus Binney
South Glamorgan Record Office
The Brecknock Museum
The Dyott Family
The Georgian Group
The late Jon James
Tom Lloyd
Tom Pollock for making the book what it is.
Tony Jukes
University of Wales, Bangor, Archives and Library
University of Wales, Cardiff, Archives and Library
Victorian Society
Will Palin

Photographic Acknowledgments

Crown copyright: Royal Commission on the Ancient and Historical Monuments of Wales: *historic images of Blaen Baglan, Boverton Place, Bronwydd, Brynglas Hall, Bwlch-Mawr, Cardiff Bay Station, Cardiff Exchange Building, Carmarthen Guildhall, Castle Green House, Foxhall Newydd, Great Frampton, Llwyn Ynn, Melai Stables, Nanteos, Nanteos Stables, Nannau, Norton Manor House, Our Lady Star of the Sea, Pencoed Castle, Plas Coch, Plas Kynaston, Plas Rhiwaedog, Plas Taliaris, Pool Park, Whitson Court.*

From the collections of the National Monuments Record of Wales: Thomas Lloyd Collection: *historic images of Baron Hill, Blaen Blodau, Edwinsford, Faenol Old Hall, Fort Hubberston, Glynllifon, Golden Grove, Gwynfryn, Hay Castle, Iscoed, Madryn Castle Gatehouse, Neuadd Fawr, Pant Glas, The Priory, Usk, Trawsgoed, Aberystwyth, Troy House, Mitchel Troy, Tyn-yr-Heol.*

Auriol, Marchioness of Linlithgow: Bryngwyn, Cardiff Library Service: Cathays Mortuary Chapels, Gary Cooper, Ceredigion County Council: Castle Green House and Cardigan Castle, Cornelia Bayley: Plas Teg and Bettisfield Park, Historic House Hotels: Bodysgallen, Louise Parker: Trevor Hall, Mike Roberts: Kinmel Park, North Wales Hospital Historical Society: North Wales Hospital, Denbigh, Pat Moseley: Ruperra Castle and Sker House, Peter and Judy Welford: Gwydir Castle, Rhyl Library Service: The Grange Hotel, Richard Wallace: Piercefield Park, Richard Watson: Insole Court, Thomas Lloyd: Tegfynydd, Temple Trust: Cilwendeg Pigeon House

Index

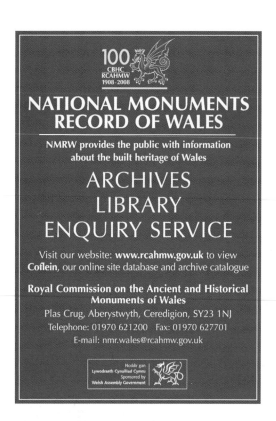

SAVE Britain's Heritage

campaigning for threatened historic buildings

SAVE Britain's Heritage is a strong, independent voice in conservation – free to respond rapidly to emergencies and to speak out for the historic environment.

SAVE was founded in 1975 to campaign publicly for endangered historic buildings. Through press releases, reports and exhibitions, SAVE has championed the cause of hundreds of decaying historic buildings, from country houses to railway stations, historic law courts to industrial mills and hospitals to farms.

From the outset, SAVE has always placed a special emphasis on the possibilities of alternative uses for historic buildings and, in a number of cases, it has prepared its own schemes for the re-use of threatened buildings.

SAVE receives no regular financial support from Government and is greatly dependent on the generosity of individuals to continue its valuable work.

You can help us save our heritage.
Please remember us in your will.

SAVE Britain's Heritage,
70 Cowcross Street, London EC1M 6EJ
Telephone: 0207 253 3500

www.savebritainsheritage.org
Registered Charity No. 269129

SAVE
BRITAIN'S HERITAGE

The Royal Commission on the Ancient and Historical Monuments of Wales - Home of the National Monuments Record of Wales

Nannerth Ganol before restoration

In its Centenary year, the Royal Commission on the Ancient and Historical Monuments of Wales has been pleased to respond to the request to provide images for this publication from its national archive of the Welsh historic environment. The book presents us with a stark reminder of the importance of recording our built heritage, whether it be a glorious mansion or a coal-blackened terrace. The Royal Commission works to do precisely that. It is now an Assembly Government Sponsored Body and is the national organisation responsible for surveying and recording archaeological and historical sites, structures, landscapes and maritime remains in Wales. It plays a leading role in developing and promoting the understanding of our built heritage through its primary survey programmes and as the originator, curator and supplier of authoritative information for individual, corporate and governmental decision makers, researchers, and the general public.

The Royal Commission's survey programmes investigate themes of national and regional interest in current archaeology, architectural and industrial history. It works closely with the local authorities to record sites that appear on their Buildings at Risk Registers and promotes the recording of listed buildings threatened with demolition or substantial alteration. It also runs an aerial photography programme documenting the landscapes of Wales from prehistory to the present. Every year the Royal Commission's aerial archaeologist discovers long-hidden sites and provides new perspectives on known monuments and buildings.

Initially the Royal Commission released the information it gathered about the historic environment through county inventories, which began with Montgomeryshire in 1910 and ended with the Later Castles of Glamorgan in 2000. Houses of the Welsh Countryside (1975; 1988) began the move from the county-based approach to the publication of national and regional studies of particular themes. This continues, alongside accessible booklets and leaflets highlighting the Royal Commission's work.

All the information gathered over the last 100 years is held in the National Monuments Record of Wales (NMRW), the Royal Commission's archive. This is the national collection of information about the historic environment of Wales, from the earliest cave dwellings to twenty-first century windfarms. It includes over 1.5 million photographs and many thousands of drawings, surveys, reports and maps. Its special collections include vertical and oblique aerial photography, historic maps, photographic albums from the last century and large collections of architectural plans. The archive grows daily as information is gathered directly through the Royal Commission's research and survey programmes and from donations of material by other organisations and private individuals. The archive can be accessed through Coflein, our online database, by visiting the library and search room or by contacting the free enquiry service.

Nannerth Ganol after restoration